Corporate Crimes & Financial Frauds

With Biggest Financial Frauds in the History of India

Corporate Crimes & Financial Frauds

With Biggest Financial Frauds in the History of India

Dr. Sumit Sharma

AUTHORSPRESS

Worldwide Circulation through Authorspress Global Network
First Published 2013
by
Authorspress

Editorial
Q-2A Hauz Khas Enclave
New Delhi-110 016

Marketing
E-35/103, Jawahar Park
Laxmi Nagar, Delhi-110 092

e-mails: authorspress@rediffmail.com; authorspress@hotmail.com
Website: www.authorspressbooks.com

Corporate Crimes & Financial Frauds
With Biggest Financial Frauds in the History of India

ISBN 978-81-7273-712-2

Printed in India at Krishna Offset, Shahdara.

सत्यमेव जयते

भारतीय प्रतिस्पर्धा आयोग

COMPETITION COMMISSION OF INDIA

Foreword

Bhopal Gas leak disaster in India was the first major corporate crime involving gross negligence by an Indian subsidiary of Union Carbide resulting into death of over twenty thousand persons and causing several ailments due to exposure to deadly gases to about 1,20,000 survivors needing constant medical attention. The manner in which this crime was handled by Indian courts exhibited the incapability of the Indian Government and the Indian Courts to handle mega-scale corporate crimes. The effort of the Indian Government was that the trial and claim of damages in respect of this crime should take place in US and for this purpose an affidavit was filed before US District Court by Attorney General of India that Indian courts were incapable of handling a case of such magnitude. After December, 1984 till date, we have not developed either the capacity or the mindset to handle big corporate crimes.

The corporate crimes have been rising in India due to the simple fact that India is a fertile ground for corporate frauds and crimes. There is absence of will power on the part of the State to protect citizens who become victims of such crimes and there is unwillingness of the courts to accept the challenge of meeting the situation and change its own mindset. Today, the courts are obsessed with personal liberties and do not mind sacrificing the interest of the society or the nation for the sake of personal liberty of a person. No legislature can think of all future events that may fall within the definition framed in respect of something. It becomes the duty and the obligation of the court to give meaningful interpretation to the provisions of law. The Courts in India have been doing this since independence and the scope of several Articles of the Constitution of India contained in the chapter of Fundamental Rights and the articles relating to personal liberty have been enlarged by the Supreme Court from time to time. However, whenever the issue of personal liberty vis-a-vis society appeared before the court, the courts have adopted the principle of strict definition and interpreted law so as to benefit the individual and courts discarded the interpretation which could have benefited the society. This mindset has resulted in a situation where people mock over Indian courts and the judicial system so much so that recently the Law Minister in a conference has stated that people consider our laws as impotent (Times of India/13.1.2013). The trial of cases of corporate frauds and corporate crimes run for decades and the state has failed to make laws to meet the situation and also failed to provide paraphernalia to curb the crimes. The result is that there is a eruption in the corporate crimes in India and new kinds of offences and new kinds of frauds emerge every day.

Lust for money has been the main cause for increase in the incidents of socioeconomic criminality; be it through evasion of taxes or avoidance of taxes or generating black money indulging in money laundering. The issue of black money has been continuously ignored and put under carpet despite there being reports of Govt. Committees and Private organisations showing the extent of black money and spread of this evil. The recent case of Vodafone is another classic example of tax evasion and the response of the court. The Supreme Court instead of going into the substance of the transaction has gone into the form of transaction despite an earlier five judges bench decision already there for curbing such a practice. Justice J.S. Verma, Retired Chief Justice of India described the decision as one of the three black judgments in the judicial history of India. The corporate frauds are encouraged in the field of tax evasion due to such decisions. Corruption and bribery of public servants, insurance frauds, bank loan frauds, racketeering in employment, illegal foreign trade, hawala transactions, credit card frauds, racketeering in false travel documents, intellectual property theft, cyber crimes, inside trading, fudging of accounts to raise market, stock market manipulations etc., etc., are prevalent and on the rise.

The corporate crimes could have been checked to a greater extent if the courts had taken a pragmatic approach in interpretation and provisions of law keeping in mind the purpose of enactment rather then saving the offender on the ground of personal liberties. The strict construction rule being adopted by the court in case of tax evasions, crimes and other statutes where there were penal liabilities of the individuals/corporate should have yielded in favour of a purposive construction or the construction to obviate the mischief. Though in case of criminal laws and taxing statutes and other penal laws, the superior courts have adopted the attitude that they have no power to add words to the language of the statute but while interpreting the provisions of the constitution and other social welfare legislations, the courts have not only enlarged the scope of the provisions but added words to the language of the statute. All penal provisions like any other statute should be interpreted so as to exhibit the legislative intent as expressed in the enactment. This view was expressed by the Supreme Court in Standard Chartered Bank vs. Directorate of Environment (AIR (2005) SC.2622) wherein the Court observed that "it is sheer violence to common sense that the legislature intended to punish the corporate bodies for minor and silly offences and extended immunity of prosecution to major and grave economic agreements." However, this purposive construction of the statute remains confined to this case only and again in Vodafone case, the court reverted back to a strict construction sticking to the form and not to the substance.

A true corporate crimes study should concentrate not only on criminality of body corporate but also on the role played by the individuals associated with it and the body corporation and individuals should be separately punished for the respective crimes. Though the Government set up a Multi Disciplinary Investigative agency called Serious Frauds Investigation office wherein experts from banking sector, capital market. Banking law, general law, forensic audit taxation, information technology work together to unravel corporate frauds, however, since 2003 when SIFO was constituted, it did not get a single court verdict in the cases it filed. Normally JPCs (Joint Parliamentary Committee) are constituted to go into certain serious frauds. However, these Committees also do not go into the issue as to which powerful politicians helped the companies to borrow recklessly and enrich themselves. The Senate Committee as constituted in US and the JPC as constituted in India both do not go into the roles of politicians who help in the corporate frauds.

With the opening up of economy by India in 1991 and India being presented as a market before the multi national companies so that they may establish their business and offices here, the responsibility of the state and the courts both to save the Indian people from corporate crimes and corporate negligence has increased. Law has to keep pace with the times and the legislative assemblies must keep on enacting new laws to meet the revolution in the nature of crimes. The advancement of technology and science is contributing to the emergence and growth of new kinds of white collar and economic crimes and the law in India must also keep pace with it. Policy makers often raise false hopes by calling for legislative response to the sensational cases as has happened in the recent gang rape case but actually doing nothing. It is for the society to ensure that policy makers and the legislature do not forget their promise. After Bhopal gas leak case & mass homicide, no law has been framed in India about culpability of companies and the individual concerned with the governance of such companies, in cases of homicides or mass homicides. However, in other countries, the legislature has already framed laws making companies responsible for mass homicide due to negligence. Similarly, there are no adequate and effective criminal laws framed for causing environmental disasters by corporations.

This is the first work by the author and he has made a good attempt on corporate crimes and financial frauds. Almost all important cases of corporate crimes in India have been dealt with in the book and the jurisprudence relating to corporate crimes has also been elaborately stated, wherever needed. The author has taken pains to unravel the principles of criminal jurisprudence and theories of corporate criminal liability. The author has specifically dealt with Bhopal Gas tragedy and other corporate crimes which had taken place in India since 1980s. He has traced the history of corporate crimes in India and has also referred to crimes like terrorism, financing, hawala, credit card frauds, balance sheet blooping. I hope the book will be useful to the advocates and the students alike.

Justice S.N. Dhingra (Retd.)

Preface

The book *Corporate Frauds and Financial Crimes* speaks about the hard reality of the new and surfacing corporate crimes and frauds of financial nature in India. The book brings out the modus used by the twenty-first century financial criminals to commit crimes and the loopholes in the system which allow them to escape the Law.

In the typical Indian set-up where ordering a simple software by a government department requires a bundle of approvals and the file has to move from various departments, it becomes challenging for the governmental machinery to compete with the minds of those equipped with sharp techniques and geeky gadgets, who are committed to carry out financial crimes.

The lack of any effective work in this field led me to research and pioneer this work. Moreover, there is no other book which deals with the issues dealt with in this book. The chapters individually deal with the *background of corporate crimes*, the concept of *corporate criminal liability*, *hawala*, *terrorist financing*, *credit card frauds*, etc. The scope and extent of Corporate Criminal Liability has been discussed in this book alongwith the laws laid down by the Hon'ble Apex Court of India in the latest landmark cases. The concept of *identity theft* is nothing new for

Europe and the USA, but the same is the sort of crime that has now been heard of in India as well. This book deals with the ways of commission of identity theft used by the criminals the world over and also the laws enacted by various countries to protect the people from such crimes.

Unfortunately, crime protection in India only happens after the crime, and criminals establish themselves and their ways. And never does it happen that our government is ready with ideas of crime prevention before its occurrence.

Among other crimes are also common the crimes committed by the members of a family in cases where the business of the family is run through a company. A chapter has been written on the Family Company Frauds, citing the instances of these frauds dealt with by me in my professional career, bringing out the loopholes in the executive and judicial system.

Dressing up of the balance sheet is one of the most common crimes which is committed every year at the time of filing of the returns and audits, in almost 95 per cent of the cases. However, this crime has the least number of convictions. The reason for it is that these returns are prepared by expert professionals and filed in connivance with the assessee himself. Also, the returns are filed in the name of the assessee and there is no attestation by any tax professional on the same. Consequently there is no proof against the person who filed the return and no criminal case is made out against the assessee or the tax professional. This issue of 'dressing up the balance sheet' has been discussed in a chapter along with the ways used by professionals to inflate and deflate the figures of the financial statements.

This book is an attempt to examine the new-age corporate crimes and financial frauds in Indian perspective, with a reference to provisions of international laws relating to such crimes.

Dr. Sumit Sharma

Introduction

India is a land of masses, a country of diversity having thousands of spoken languages, newspapers, cultures, religions, gods and goddesses, and foods in its 28 states and seven union territories. A country where scandals are forgotten as quickly as are the sorrows. Where a scam only lasts till the morning cup of tea for a common man. A country where the development is keeping its pace, but does it really reach the society at large, is the primary question. The growing flyways, shopping malls, toll plazas have brought more traffic, more tolls and more inflating prices with them.

I remember my economics professor commenting in our lecture, about a decade ago, "Consumerism shall make this country a slave of desire one day." Well, I can now relate to his foresight of the future. We actually have become more consumerist than ever. And consumerism leads us to believe, certain behavioural patterns, as being moral and legal, which may not be moral or legal otherwise. For example parents these days are ready to pay almost any amount to get their child admitted to the posh schools of the metros. Or we may be ready to buy a train or airplane ticket on a premium which is absolutely not required to be paid. The short-lived memory of the majority chunk of India, that is, the common man, is so used to forgetting things. Take the instance of the VIP number registration scandal in Delhi. A guy running a canteen in the government authority had countless number of cars and all with a single-digit VVIP numbers, which were actually meant for VIPs. And when the scam was busted by the media, the common man just remembered it for a few days and then the car registrations for VIP numbers were routed through Haryana and Chandigarh.

The price of petrol which was Rs. 44 in the year 2009 reached Rs. 78 in 2012. Are we really progressing or just dragging the economy? Amidst all the scams happening in the government and the doors of apex court being knocked every day for justice, this country has still a lot of potential in terms of capable buyers, large and extensive market for products.

Writing this book on corporate frauds and financial crimes has not been a difficult task, if I accept honestly, since India is a growing country and along with it are growing the novel ways of committing the crimes. However, the techniques and suggestions for preventing such crimes has been really difficult. Especially in the current legal scenario of our country, where recently an accused standing outside a court told me, "The case has been going on for so long that I've forgotten whether I'm really innocent or guilty".

It's amazing how my research has led me to believe in the fact that the age-old saying has claimed over the years "All that glitters is not gold". What a corporate entity appears to a commoner may not be the true depiction of its character, as even the mirror would only reflect what is placed in front of it and not what is behind.

Corporate criminals are not different from the usual cheats, swindlers and frauds, rather only their identity is the point of contrast. My curiosity for knowing the origin of corporate criminals led me to know a few benefits of the newly arrived corporate crime in the modern socioeconomics scene in India.

Being able to get away only with fines rather imprisonment, huge money, no individual trials, complexity of investigation and lack of effective law were the few big attractions for this form of crime.

India has had one of the poorest conviction rates in cases of corporate frauds, and such cases taking years before they finally get decided. In comparison, a corporate fraud task force set up by US President George W. Bush in 2002, secured 1,236 convictions in five years. Among those held guilty included the top officials of Enron and World Com companies. In the UK, the serious frauds office has an average conviction rate of 61 per cent in frauds cases during the past few years.

In India, in order to streamline the prosecution system of the country, the ministry of company affairs set up a committee in 2005 under the Companies Act. The failure to categorise cases and give priority to cases of serious frauds is clogging the courts and leading to huge delays, it said. While pointing out major flaws in the existing system, it recommended withdrawal of petty cases, separate courts for cases of serious frauds and a time limit to decide these cases. Well, as expected, none of the recommendations have been implemented so far.

In view of the above, I have tried to concise the kinds of modern-day corporate crimes with the most famous corporate crimes committed. Maybe I will leave you wondering about the explorations of these crimes in the Indian scenario.

Contents

1

Corporate and Financial Crimes: A Background

In a country like India, where a man as popular as Baba Ramdev was literally thrown out of New Delhi, when he was trying to protest peacefully against corruption, the author really had to think before coming out with his views in the form of this book. This book contains financial and corporate laws and crimes and criminals related to them. But he holds himself here to accept what one wise man always said, "Existence of laws is one thing, and their implementation is something another, something very difficult."

The fact of lack of implementation is much evident from the fact that the apex court of India had to exercise the scope of judicial review to its fullest, letting the government know the supremacy of the rule of law, may it be the quashing of the appointment of the CVC, or monitoring of the 2G spectrum matter, or prevention of mass spoilage of foodgrains happening in the godowns of Food Corporation of India (especially when millions of souls sleep without food at night in our country). The courts have really taken the task in their hand, and it has been in the best of interests of the country and its citizens.

A burning example of the systematic injustice was seen when a child suffering from cancer was denied treatment by most of the better government hospitals in New Delhi. The only respite to the child came when his father filed a petition with the court in New Delhi, asking for a basic right to get treated and for medical help. And no prize for guessing that he was provided that right by the orders of the court.

India has diversity, and diversity creates confusion. Confusion not qua making the laws, but for its implementation. A lot of implementation has happened in tPrinted in India at Krishna Offset, Shahdara.he years 2009, 2010 and 2011, for the good of the country.

Apart from the usual crimes, now have evolved the white collar crimes, which are more difficult to detect since they are the result of well trained brains. In corporates the deterrence of illegal acts and fraud requires coordinated efforts by the management, audit committee and auditors. Falsification of books of accounts constitutes fraud and illegal act.

Besides illegal acts, corporate frauds can fall into two categories—one leading to falsification of accounting records and the other misappropriation of assets or fraudulent expenditures. Fraud analysts find three causal factors constituting a triangle in all frauds. The best way to reduce the occurrence of fraud is strengthening the internal control system. Although the Association of Certified Fraud Examiners and National Association of Certified Valuation Analysts have also elaborated effective controls to deter fraud, yet still most of the companies have no anti-fraud policies. A multi-pronged strategy to take action to prevent corporate frauds when organisations are expanding beyond borders, and systems and procedures, become complex, the management needs to be more vigilant.

Identification of the fraud vulnerability and actions to detect, control and prevent control deficiencies for effective enterprise risk management by reducing the likelihood of susceptibilities are important in this century.

The financial crimes are nothing new. They have existed since ages. For this century, the story started with early 2000, when the infamous *Enron* moved away from its core business of electricity and natural gas towards trading in derivatives. It believed that the profits from derivatives could be used to mask the losses of its primary business. Enron started incurring massive debts. Though its derivatives related asset yields grew by good numbers, liabilities also piled up rapidly. The trouble began in 2001. Enron created multiple Special Purpose Vehicles to hide bad investments in derivatives as well as its poorly performing assets in the energy business.[1]

It started avoiding millions in tax dues by using its stock options. Its financial condition was sustained by institutionalised, systematic and creatively planned accounting fraud. In the meantime it lost exclusive rights to its pipelines.

For the third quarter of 2001, it reported a huge $618 million loss, and on November 4, 2001 it told its investors that they were restating profits for the last four and a quarter years. Finally, on December 2, 2001 the company filed for bankruptcy. The scandal created such waves in the auditing community that it led to the dissolution of Arthur Andersen, one of the world's top accounting firms.

Followed by Enron was WorldCom scandal. WorldCom was the United States second largest long-distance phone operator between 1998 and 2002. During the 1990s, WorldCom was involved in acquisitions and completed several "mega-deals" which later turned out detrimental. In the year 1999, revenue growth stalled. The company started borrowing money to cover up losses. By March 2002, the Securities and Exchange Commission (SEC) requested for information from WorldCom, suspecting fraud, as AT&T was losing money even as WorldCom wasn't. What was feared came to be true when, in July, the company announced bankruptcy and later that month it declared that it had been inflating profits by $3.8 billion over the previous five quarters. The company inflated profits by classifying routine expenses as investments and long-term expenses, it also capitalised "line costs"—fees paid to third party operators to carry traffic.

Not much after the Worldcom scandal shook the financial market, the office equipment-maker, Xerox, in June 2002, admitted to overstating its revenues and profits for the years 1997-2001. This allowed the company to meet profit expectations. When SEC began an investigation, it exposed the fact that over five years the company had improperly classified over $6 billion in revenue, leading to an overstatement of earnings by nearly $2 billion.

The popular internet service provider America Online (AOL) was accused of playing around with its finances in the early 1990s. In these years, changing its amortisation policies and capitalizing revenue expenses was a commonly followed practice in US. The magnitude of fraud began to increase with competition. And from March 2000 through January 2002, the company indulged in material misstatements of its financial results, including overstatements of operating income and free cash flow, overstatements of net income, understatements of net losses and total debt. The intention was to report that it had met its new subscriber targets, an important metric the market used to evaluate AOL. The bigger loss had fallen on someone else, since in the meanwhile Times Warner had taken over AOL. This resulted in Time Warner paying $300 million to SEC as civil penalties.

According to a report dated March 18, 2008 by KPMG, Corporate India is unprepared to handle fraud.

India is perceived as a fraud-haven with inadequacy of anti-fraud measures and unethical behaviour of employees. The

- Over 70 percent corporates believe fraud in India will increase over next two years.
- Supplier kickback most prevalent form of fraud to hit an organization.
- Theft of Intellectual Property and IT-related fraud will increase in coming years.
- Organizations lack effective internal control mechanisms to manage risks.

dual impact of two concerns rated high by respondents, i.e., unethical behaviour of employees and inadequacy of anti-fraud measures, leads to an environment where both inclination and opportunity co-exist. This could mean that organizations in India that remain passive in their approach to deal with fraud may be a perfect breeding ground for fraud, suggests the findings of the latest KPMG report on fraud.

The findings of the KPMG report suggest that the threat of fraud comes mostly from within the organization. A majority of the respondents believe that the employees pose the maximum threat to an organization and the senior management as compared to other employees is more likely to commit fraud. The inherent responsibilities and trust associated with senior positions the ability to override internal controls, internal knowledge and access to confidential company information that come with the managerial position create the risk that fraudulent acts may occur. Next to employees the maximum threat is perceived from suppliers and service providers. Hence it is not surprising to know that the collusion between the two would be a major area of concern.

Supplier kickbacks is the most prevalent type of fraud being faced by the organizations today. The KPMG report highlights that typically companies refrain from taking legal action against fraud perpetrators and prefer separating the perpetrator of fraud from the company (employees) or stop dealing with them (external parties). Action taken by organizations greatly depends upon their outlook and tolerance towards fraud as well as their appetite to deal with law enforcement and legal channels, should they choose to prosecute perpetrators.

The concept of corporate criminal liability and the limit thereof has not been defined by the legislature anywhere. The gap between the legislation and the corporate criminal brains has widened ever since. It has become more common than ever these days, that whenever a big corporate crime has been committed, it is only done under the garb of a corporate mask. I have concised the judicial view taken by the courts on the limits of corporate liability, in another chapter on Corporate Criminal Liability.

The number of deaths which take place during an year on account of various crimes is usually accounted for by the police agencies. However, the deaths which are the result of corporate crimes are never accounted for. These include deaths of labour occurred while construction of big commercial and residential complexes by builders, deaths of consumers caused due to faulty products of companies, corporate pollution and not to forget deaths and cancers caused by sale of tobacco and paan masala. Sadly, India has no figures regarding the death toll on account of these corporate deaths.

However, there is some data available with the US Department of Justice, which has explained in its 2001-2006 strategic plan, that "precise financial losses resulting from White Collar Crime (WCC) for consumers, government, and business are unknown since no systematic data collection exists."[2]

Corporations also cause more violence and death than street criminals. The US national murder rate reported by the FBI is about 13,000 for the year 2011.[3] Compare that to the number of people who die from corporate-related causes each year:

a) According to the Bureau of Labor Statistics' annual report on workplace fatalities, 4,547 people died on the job in USA in the year 2010. This preliminary number is slightly lower than the 4,551 fatal injuries recorded in 2009, and the lowest on record since the Bureau of Labor Statistics began tracking this information in 1992.

b) Another study estimates that 70,000 Americans die annually from product-related accidents, and millions more suffer disabling injuries at a cost of over $100 billion in property damage, lost wages, insurance, litigation, and medical expenses.[4] Despite improved regulations, the Consumer Product Safety Commission estimates that "there remain 27,100 deaths and 33.1 million injuries each year" related to consumer products under its jurisdiction.

c) These numbers do not include the thousands of annual deaths caused by cancer and other diseases linked to corporate pollution, defective products, tainted food and addictive substances such as tobacco, and other causes. An estimated 553,400 people in the US died from cancer in 2001 (See J. NCI: 93:10, *Stat Bite*, May 6, 2001).

As the need of today, corporate criminal responsibility must be fixed and enforced in an effective manner to plug the hole of corporate criminal leakage from the hands of law. Concepts like corporate governance[5] seem attractive when discussed in board meetings or investor seminars. They actually don't exist in the real world for the purposes of private limited companies. The situation in privately owned companies is more complex than in the PSUs and the MNCs where there are clearly defined dominant shareholders. In the Indian business groups, the concept of dominant shareholders is more amorphous for two reasons. First, the promoters' shareholding is spread across several friends and relatives as well as corporate entities. It is sometimes difficult to establish the total effective holding of this group. Second, the aggregate holding of all these entities taken together is typically well below a majority stake. In many cases, the promoter may not even be the largest single shareholder. What makes the promoters the dominant shareholders is that a large chunk of the shares is held by state-owned financial institutions which have historically played a passive role. So passive have they been that in the few cases where they did become involved in corporate governance issues, they were widely seen as acting at the behest of their political masters and not in pursuance of their financial interests.

In comparison with developed countries that impose stringent penal and criminal consequences for poor corporate governance, penalty levels in India are considered to be inadequate to enforce good governance. Greater efforts are still required to stop the corporate crimes being committed. And that can only be achieved with effective legislation on corporate crimes and fixation of liability of corporate offenders.

Notes and References

1. S. Hamsini Amritha, Corporate frauds over the years, *Business Line,* 11.1.09.
2. http://www.corporatepolicy.org/issues/crimedata.htm (Center for Corporate Policy, Washington, DC).

3. http://www.fbi.gov/about-us/cjis/ucr/crime-in-the-u.s/2010/crime-in-the-u.s.-2010/tables/10shrtbl01.xls.
4. Brobeck and Averyt, *The Product Safety Book*, New York: Dutton, 1983, reported in David O. Friedrichs, *Trusted Criminals: White Collar Crime in Contemporary Society*, Belmont, CA: Wadsworth Publishing, 1996.
5. Corporate governance is characterized by a firm commitment and adoption of ethical practices by an organization across its entire value chain and in all of its dealings with a wide group of stakeholders encompassing employees, customers, vendors, regulators and shareholders (including the minority shareholders), in both good and bad times. To achieve this, certain checks and practices need to be whole-heartedly embraced.(http://www.in.kpmg.com/tl_files/pictures/cg%20survey%20report.pdf).

2

Financial Crimes by Companies

A few decades ago, thinking that a company could have a mind and that it could be held guilty of some offence based on its mental state would sound a bit funny. But then time has really changed. The debate on attributing criminal liability to companies is far from over. However, there has been some light thrown on the jurisprudence on this subject by the international and Indian courts. To say that a company is totally a legal person and does not has a mind of its own, and thereby guilt cannot be imposed on it would be wrong in the present context. With the changing world, the operations of the companies have grown immensely. And to be seen in true sense the companies are actually run by a bunch of living people only. So the mind of those decision-making persons is really the mind of the company itself.

This cannot be limited to the famous case of Salomon vs. Salomon,[1] i.e., 'lifting the corporate veil of the company' in the present scenario. Since then ages have passed and ever more evolved are the novel ways of committing financial crimes.

In criminal jurisprudence, every crime has to follow a motive, a purpose, or intent that indicates the presence of a criminal state of mind, i.e., the *mens rea*. The Indian Penal Code (IPC) in section 81, deals with the concept of mens rea (the criminal state of mind) as the basic ingredient behind any offence.

However, the concept of *mens rea* becomes extremely complex in case of corporate acts, since it is extremely difficult to attach a particular intent to a company at a particular point of time, it being a mere group of different human beings. Now the question which gains significance is whether a company could have guilty mind at all. And if NO then, whether the concept of "no *mens rea*, no crime" will be applicable to the financial crimes committed by the companies.

The view in favour of corporate criminal liability advocates that companies are not mere fictions. They exist and occupy a predominant position within the society, and are as capable as human beings of causing harm. It is only just and consistent with the principle of equality before the law to treat them like natural persons and hold them liable for the offences they commit.

The need for corporate criminal liability has arisen because of the ever-increasing shift of the crimes being committed by individuals, to the white collar crimes committed by companies. The English courts had started sentencing the corporates for financial crimes in the middle of the last century, although many of the European continental law countries have not been able to incorporate provisions to create a corporate criminal liability even of late.

"Financial planning requires long-term thinking. Especially if you get caught."

Much of the jurisprudence of the corporate criminal liability has gained its shape from the number of while collar crimes, ever increasing and never ending. The evolvement of the theories of corporate criminal liability has been a twentieth century development, influenced by "sweeping expansion" of the common law principles.[2]

Now again the principal question needs to be answered, whether the corporate entity can take a criminal state of mind (i.e. *mens rea*). The decision of the Mumbai High Court[3] in this context clarifies that in case of imposition of penalties for defaults, *mens rea* is not an essential element and cannot be pleaded as defence.

In the above case, CICC, an American company, held 51 per cent in an Indian subsidiary, Cabot India Ltd (CIL), listed on the Bombay Stock Exchange. CIL sought to make a preferential issue to CICC, subject to regulatory and statutory approvals. In early February 1997, the FIPB and RBI approvals were obtained and the stock exchanges were informed.

In the meantime, the SEBI Takeover Code 1997 came into operation on 22 February. In April 1997, the allotment took place, pursuant to a special resolution under Section 81 (IA) of the Companies Act. In November 1998, while considering exemption for a public offer by CICC in relation to a further acquisition, SEBI took the view that CICC ought to have filed the report of the acquisition with details of shareholding under Regulations 3 (4) and (5) of the 1997 Takeover Code. CICC's stand on the matter was that virtually all formalities had been complied with before the 1997 Takeover Code became operative and the non-compliance was unintentional. Admittedly, however, a report was submitted by CICC after a delay of 530 days. The Adjudicating Officer, SEBI, investigating the matter on consideration, imposed a penalty of Rs 1.5 lakh on CICC.

CICC challenged the order by way of appeal before the SEBI Appellate Tribunal (SAT) on the ground that there was no deliberate dis-regard of the Takeover Code; the default, if any, was without *mens rea* and had not affected any investors' interests, adversely or otherwise. The 1997 Regulations were not retrospective and therefore not applicable. SAT allowed the appeal as in its view CICC had not acted deliberately or contumaciously in defiance of law.

Before the Appeal Court, several precedents were cited on the issue of *mens rea*. The substance of the submissions, and the finding in law that followed were that while *mens rea* is essential for a criminal offence, it cannot be blindly applied to be a condition precedent to each and every case. The Appeal Court has relied on the Supreme Court Constitution Bench judgment in RS Joshi vs Ajit Mills, that the classical view "no *mens rea*, no crime" has been eroded in India and abroad, particularly in the case of economic crimes and regulatory penalties, which in the present case was a civil obligation. That clearly ruled out *mens rea* as a concept although the Appeal Court did agree with the SAT's finding on the factual matrix. This was strange, since the Regulation (3)(1)(c) clearly refers to preferential allotments being made pursuant to a special resolution. Both events took place after the 1997 Regulation became operative.

The fact clearly brought out though, that an act attracting penalty (even if it is unintentional) cannot be condoned.

Generally, companies may be held criminally responsible for the illegal acts of its employees if such acts are related to and committed within the course of employment, committed in furtherance of the business of the company and its imbibed culture.

Theories of Corporate Criminal Liability

The theories of attributing criminal liability to financial crimes committed by companies have been evolved with the occurrence of such incidents over the years. They are the result of various decisions and rulings of the courts of law, internationally.

I have discussed them briefly in this chapter to give an overview of the basis of corporate criminal liability.

The Agency Theory/ Doctrine of Vicarious Liability

The traditional theory of vicarious liability holds the master liable for the acts of the servant in the course of the master's business without proof of any personal fault on the part of the master.

According to this theory, the company is held liable for the acts of its employees. Vicarious liability (or respondeat superior) is commonly employed in the United States. In other jurisdictions, this theory is restrictively established in relation to some strict liability and hybrid offences that deal with matters such as pollution, food, drugs, health and safety at work but not to *mens rea* offences.

The doctrine of vicarious liability is based on the premise that criminal violations normally entail two elements, *actus reus* and *mens rea*. Since companies are considered to be purely incorporeal legal entities, they do not posses any mental state and the only way to impute intent to a company is to consider the state of mind of its employees. The theory has a simple and logical method of attributing liability to a corporate offender: if companies do not have intention, someone within the companies must have it, and the intention of this individual as part of the company is the intention of the company itself. Courts in the United States, where this theory is widely used, have developed a *three-tier* test to determine whether a company will be held vicariously liable for the acts of its employees.

Firstly, the employee must be acting *within the scope and course of his employment*. Secondly, the employee must be acting, at least in part, *for the benefit of the company*, yet it is irrelevant whether the company actually receives the benefit or whether the activity might even have been expressly prohibited. Thirdly, *the act and intent must be imputed to the company*.[4]

Scope of employment

The requirement that an employee must be acting within the scope of his or her employment is met if the employee has actual or apparent authority to engage in the act in question.[5] Actual authority exists when a company knowingly and intentionally authorizes an employee to act on its behalf.

In New York Central Railroad,[6] it was the first Supreme Court case holding a corporation criminally liable. The corporation was convicted of violating the Elkins Act where a general and an assistant traffic manager paid rebates for shipments of sugar. The agents acted within the scope of actual authority because they were authorized to set up freight rates. Therefore, they acted within the scope of authority conferred upon them by the company.

In United States v. Investment Enters., Inc.,[7] the company was convicted of violating obscenity laws where the company's president conspired to transport obscene videos in interstate commerce. The president's unlawful acts could be imputed to the company because he was an "undisputedly authorized agent."

The question of whether an employee acted in the scope of his or her authority is differently determined by each source of law and factual framework. Federal courts have constantly held that a company may be liable for the actions of its agents regardless of the agent's position within the company. These courts have found that an employee's act can bind the company even where the company has implemented policies prohibiting the behaviour. When an employee's conduct is contrary to the company's compliance policies and specific directives, the company can still be held liable.[8] The company can prove that it has established corporate policies in an effort to reduce crime, but this does not prevent a court from finding it criminally liable. The existence of an effective compliance policy will not provide an absolute defence from criminal liability,[9] but the company may qualify for a reduced penalty.

Benefiting the Company

The second element of corporate criminal liability according to the theory of vicarious liability is that the act benefits the company. The benefit need not be real, yet potential. As Hall points out, "For this requirement, the corporation need not actually receive a benefit; the employee's mere intention to bestow a benefit suffices."[10]

It is not necessary that the employee be primarily concerned with benefiting the corporation since many employees act primarily for their own personal gain. Although the corporation did not actually gain from the action or the agent violated a company policy, liability may still be imputed to a corporation.

The above two aspects along with the fact that the act and intent of the employee is being imputed o the company, would impose vicarious liability on the company.

Vicarious Liability in Indian Context

A recent judgment of the Hon'ble Supreme Court in *K.K. Ahuja* v. *V.K. Vohra*, (2009) 10 SCC 48, deals with vicarious liability under section 141 of the Negotiable Instruments Act. The Supreme Court went on to observe:

> It is evident that a person who can be made vicariously liable..... is a person who is responsible to the company for the conduct of the business of the company and in addition is also in charge of the business of the company. There may be many directors and secretaries who are not in charge of the business of the company at all... a person may be a director and thus belongs to the group of persons making the policy followed by the company, but yet may not be in charge of the business of the company; that a person may be a Manager who is in charge of the business but may not be in overall charge of the business; and that a person may be an officer who may be in charge of only some part of the business.

Thus, what emerges from the decision of the Supreme Court is that the test to be employed in determining vicarious liability is functional, and that the position of the person within the organisation cannot be conclusive always.

The Identification Theory

This theory contemplates an identity between the company and the persons who constitute its directing mind. These individuals are those whose duties within the company are such that, in the course of their duties, they do not take orders or directives from a higher authority within the organization. The commission of an offence by such person or group of persons is identified with the organization, and constitutes an offence by the company as well. The identification doctrine being developed out of the perceived need to hold companies liable for *mens rea* offences has created a pragmatic median between the extremes of total vicarious liability for all criminal acts on one hand and no corporate liability unless expressly authorized criminal acts on the other hand. This doctrine stipulates that the actions and mental stage of the company is found in the actions and state of mind of employees or officers of the company, who may be considered the directing mind and will of the company.

In most countries, the companies are held liable under the doctrine of identification under the principles of the common law. The construction of direct liability theory was due to the limitations of the agency theory. The theory was developed as an attempt to overcome the problem of imposing primary (as opposed to vicarious) corporate criminal liability for offences that insisted on proof of criminal fault.

Viscount Haldane brought out[11] a model of primary corporate criminal liability for offences that required mens rea as a pre-condition. In the light of Haldane's judgment:

> A corporation is an abstraction. It has no mind of its own any more than it has a body of its own; its active and directing will must consequently be sought in the person of somebody, who for some purposes may be called an agent, but who is really the directing mind and will of the corporation; the very ego and centre of the personality of the corporation.

As in the agency theory, the identification theory relies on an individual to attribute liability to a company. However, while the former doctrine simply imitates tort principles, the latter adjusts these principles to the reality of corporate misconduct. Furthermore, the identification theory introduces the personification of the corporate body. This theory brought out the solution for the 'problem of attributing fault to a company for offences that require intention' by merging the individual within the company with the company itself. Unlike the agency theory, the individual employee is assumed to be acting as the company and not for the company. The theory de-emphasized the need for the development of vicarious liability. The agency theory has now been considered as unjust and lacking in defensible penal rationale.

Guilty Mind

The`main underlying principle of the identification theory is the detection of the guilty mind, the recognition of the individual who will be identified as the company itself, who will be the company's very ego, vital organ, or mind.

The question is whether the manager of the company could be identified with the company via the common law doctrine, or in other words, whether a natural person or persons are to be treated as being the company itself.

Lord Denning in Botton Engineering Company Ltd. vs. Grahm and Sons (1957, 1 QB 15) 9 CA), had observed that "a company, in many cases is linked to a human body. It has a brain and a nerve centre, which controls what it does. It has also hands, which hold the tools and act in accordance with directions from the Cenozoic. Some of the people in the company are mere servants and agents, who are nothing more than hands to do the work, and cannot be said to represent the mind or will. Others are directors and managers who represent the directing mind or will of the company and control what it does. The state of mind of these managers is the state of mind of the company and is treated by the law as such."

The Doctrine of Direct Liability (Theory of Corporate Organs)

This doctrine, which was specifically developed for the purpose of imposing liability on companies, seeks, in fact, to imitate the imposition of criminal liability on human beings. The direct doctrine relies on the notion of personification of the legal body. It identifies actions and thought patterns of certain individuals within the company called corporate organs who act within the scope of their authority and on behalf of the corporate body, as the behaviour of the legal body itself. Hence, the name of the doctrine: the *theory of corporate organs* or the *alter ego doctrine* referring to these individuals as the embodiment of the legal body. In its pursue the company can be rendered criminally liable for the very perpetration of the offences, resembling the liability imposed on a human perpetrator, though subject to the natural limitations that follow from the character of the company as a legal personality.

But, the procedure to prove a company criminally liable is indeed rather complex. If intention, knowledge or recklessness is an essential ingredient of the offence, these fault ingredients must be attributed to the body corporate if it expressly, tacitly or impliedly authorized or permitted the commission of the offence. First, the company's fault will be established (vicarious liability) if the body corporate's board of directors intentionally, knowingly or recklessly carried out the wrongful conduct, or expressly or by necessary implication authorized or permitted the commission of the offence. Second, the company's fault may be established by evidence that a high managerial agent of the company intentionally, knowingly or recklessly engaged in the relevant conduct or expressly, tacitly or impliedly authorized or permitted the commission of the offence. However, in the second case the company will not be liable if it proves that it exercised due diligence to prevent the conduct. Third, the company's fault may be established by proving that it failed to create and maintain a corporate culture that required compliance with the laws of the country, or the proof that the corporate culture existed within the body corporate that encouraged, tolerated or led to non-compliance of the legal responsibility.

Assessment of the Criminal Liability: Whether Personal or Corporate?

Considering the above theories, in context of the recent and famous scandal of Satyam Computers and the owner, M.R. Raju's act of cheating and criminal breach of trust, against the company and its investors, the principal question which arises is that 'whether the liability has to be fastened on Mr Raju as an individual *or* the company itself *or* on others (in the company) who were aware of the fraud being committed'.

The concept of corporate criminal liability requires decision based on the factual matrix in such cases. The legal jurisprudence needs to determine that whether it could be justified that where a multi-thousand crore scam is committed by a company and hard earned money of lakhs of investors is taken away. But the liability is fastened merely on an individual thereby rescuing all other culprits from the paws of legal provisions. Or whether it would make sense to send a person to jail when he has caused immense loss to the innocent investors of the company or system should be made to recover the lost money? What legal remedy can give relief to people who suffered losses. Well, the answer to this is more difficult in the Indian context, since after the Satyam scam occurred, investigating agencies arrested few of the officers of the company including the Chairman, Mr Raju, even if the fraud was committed by the company as whole on its investors. This whole issue brings out the statutory inadequacy of the Indian legal system.

Statutory Inadequacy in India

The law in India still holds the theory of holding the officials responsible for the crime rather than the company itself. The Indian Penal Code incorporates various sections making compulsory imprisonment for the officers of the company, since the company itself cannot be sent to jail. Certain sections of the Companies Act like the section 45, 63, 68, 70(5), 203, etc.

wherein only the officials of the company are held liable and not the company itself, whereas certain restrictive penal provisions, entailing fine for the illegal acts, wherein a fine has been imposed on the companies when they are found to be guilty are present in following statutes:

Section 141 of the Negotiable Instruments Act, 1862

> Offences by companies: If the person committing an offence under section 138 is a company, *every person who, at the time the offence was committed, was in charge of, and was responsible to, the company for the conduct of the business* of the company, *as well as the company*, shall be deemed to be guilty of the offence and shall be liable to be proceeded against and punished accordingly: Provided that nothing contained in this sub- section shall render any person liable to punishment if he proves that the offence Was committed without his knowledge, or that he had exercised all due diligence to prevent the commission of such offence.
>
> (2) Notwithstanding anything contained in sub- section (1), where any offence under this Act has been committed by a company and it is proved that the offence has been committed with the consent or connivance of, or is attributable to, any neglect on the part of, any director, manager, secretary or other officer of the company, such director, manager, secretary or other officer shall also be deemed to be guilty of that offence and shall be liable to be proceeded against and punished accordingly.

Section 276-B & 276BB of the Income Tax Act

> If a person fails to pay to the credit of the Central Government....
>
> ....he shall be punishable with rigorous imprisonment for a term which shall not be less than three months but which may extend to seven years and with fine.

3. Section 27 of the Securities & Exchange Board of India Act

> This provision is almost identical to the section 141 of the Negotiable Instruments Act, 1862.

Problems with regard to corporate punishment arose when the courts faced situations where the criminal statutes were to be strictly applied. But the offence was committed by companies, and most punishments of the Indian Penal Code only provide for imprisonment, whereas a company cannot be imprisoned. It was hard to impose fine in lieu of imprisonment, even through the definition of "Person" in the IPC includes a 'Company'. Efforts of the Indian legislature on this issue also failed, when the bill proposing the fine as an alternate to imprisonment was not passed in 1972, and lapsed.

The Law Commission in its 41st Report also suggested following amendment to the IPC: "In every case in which the offence is only punishable with imprisonment or with imprisonment and fine and the offender is a company or other body corporate or an association of individuals, it shall be competent to the Court to sentence such offender to fine only".

Through much has not changed in the statutory part of law, but the courts have taken a strict view that the corporate bodies cannot be exonerated from being prosecuted and the intent of the legislature is always to prosecute the offender corporate body.

Precedents like the Uphaar Cinema case and the Satyam Computer's case have set the legal viewpoint in motion. But, a significant change needs to be made regarding the legislative part of the law since there is no provision in the Indian law to hold the company liable for Criminal Acts and prosecute the company itself for fine instead of imprisonment.

The well known maxim 'judicis est just dicere, non dare' best expounds the role of the court. It is to interpret the law, not to make it. This read with the Doctrine of Separation of Powers has bound the court's hands in imposing various kinds of punishments.

All that the courts are left with is to impose fines. In order to avoid compelling circumstances where the courts go out of the way to interpret and define the law, which is essentially the task of the legislature.[12] In my opinion it is advisable that the legislature amends the various penal statutes in a way so as to make various forms of punishments applicable for companies as well, thereby maintaining the separation of powers and hence the rule of law.

What Change can the Legislature Bring?

A fine can be effective punishment for minor offences, but where the offence is grave, it would be seriously questionable whether fine alone would serve the purpose of punishment. So to say, with huge amounts of black money with the Richer bit of the society, they can easily get away paying the fine, whereas the poor may not be is a position to pay any kind of fine. But where we are talking of the corporate liability (i.e., big financial crimes) fine may not even be a problem for the corporate offenders with heavy bank balances.

The legal system of formulating new laws, keeping pace with the latest developments of crime in the modern day world, needs to be vigilant and ever changing. Else, the country of enormous brain banks may turn into land of economics miscreants.

Effectively, the legislature (or the government) may consider the following changes in case of serious financial crimes:

a) Heavy compensation to the victim and in case of non compliance by the company, a compulsory sale of company's and director's assets.

b) Compulsory winding up of the company with effective mechanism to avoid any kind of delaying tactics by the company. (Although there is a provision in company's Act, 1956 with regard to winding up but the same can take immense time and is required to go through a series of legal forums which makes Compulsory winding up an ineffective remedy)

c) Life time ban on the directors of the company from being engaged in any kind of gainful employment, in case where directors/ officers of the company are found guilty.

d) Rigorous imprisonments for the offender officers and directors of the company.

In view of imposing role of companies in the economic, political and social spheres, the legal jurisdictions around the world are thinking in a similar manner towards imposing criminal liability on companies.

Although, various jurisdictions world over, have given this a statutory status, India still lacks an effective statutory system of fixing liability to criminal acts committed in the guise of company's blanket.

Notes and References

1. In the said case, owner of a business sold it to a company he had formed, in return for fully paid-up shares to himself and members of his family, and secured debentures. The company went into liquidation, the owner, because of the ownership of the debentures, won his claim to be paid off in priority to other creditors, as the secured debt ranked at a higher priority to those debts and successfully proved that he did not have to indemnify the company in respect of its debts, as it had a separate legal personality. The House of Lords lifted the corporate veil and held that in exceptional circumstances the corporate face of the company has to be pierced and the actual persons behind the legal facade have to be seen.

2. Harvey L.Pitt and Karl A Groskaufmanis, "Minimizing Corporate civil & Criminal Liability : A Second Look at corporate codes of Conduct" (1990) 78 *The Georgetown Law Journal* 1560 at 15660.
3. SEBI V/S Cabot International Capital Corporate (CLCC) [2004] 51 SCL 307 (BOM)
4. United States v. One Parcel of Land, 965 F. 2d 311, 316 (7th Cir. 1992) (stating agent's knowledge of illegal act may be imputed to corporation if agent was "acting as authorized and motivated at least in part by an intent to benefit the corporation" [citing Zero v. United States, 459 U.S. 991 (1982)].
5. United States v. Investment Enter Inc., 10 F. 3d 263, 266 (5th Cir.1993) (stating that a corporation is criminally liable for the unalwful acts of its agents, provided that the conduct is within the scope of the agent's authority, whether actual or apparent); Meyers v. Bennet Law Offices, 238 F. 3d 1068, 1073 (9th Cir 2001) (rejecting fact that employee acted outside scope of authority because employee had at least apparent authority to take actions).
6. New Hampshire v. Zeta Chi Fraternity, 696 A. 2d 530, 535 (N.H. 1997).
7. United States v. Investment Enter Inc., 10 F. 3d 263, 266 (5th Cir.1993).
8. United States v. Automated Med. Labs., Inc., 770 F. 2d 399, 407 (4th Cir. 1985) ('The fact that many of [employees'] actions were unlawful and contrary to corporate policy does not absolve [defendant] of legal responsibility for their acts").
9. Dan K. Webb et al., "Understanding and Avoiding Corporate and Executive Criminal Liability," (1994) 49 Bus Law 617 at 624 cited in Matthew E. Beck & Matthew E. O'Brien, "Corporate Criminal Liability (annual white collar crime survey)"(2000) 37 *American Law Review* 261 at 268, n.37.
10. Joseph Hall "Corporate Criminal Liability (Thirteenth Survey of White Collar Crime)" (1998) 35 American Criminal Law Review 549 at 554. Zero v. United States, 689 F. 2d 238, 242 (1st Cir. 1982) (holding that employee must have been "motivated at least in part by an intent to benefit the corporation.")
11. Carrying Co Ltd v. Asiatic Petroleum Co Ltd [1915] AC 70510.
12. Asif Hameed and others v. State of Jammu& Kashmir, AIR 1989 SC 1899.

3

Corporate Criminal Liability: Judicial Perspectives

The basic rule of criminal liability revolves around the basic Latin maxim *actus non facit reum, nisi mens sit rea.* It means that to make one liable it must be shown that act or omission has been done which was forbidden by law and has been done with guilty mind. Hence, every crime has two elements one physical one known as *actus reus* and other mental one known as *mens rea.*[1] This is the rule of criminal liability in technical sense but in general the principle upon which responsibility is premised is autonomy of the individual, which states that the imposition of responsibility upon an individual flows naturally from the freedom to make rational choices about actions and behaviours.[2] Although the general rule as stated above is applicable to all criminal cases but the criminal law jurisprudence has seen one exception to the above-said concept in the form of doctrine of strict liability, in which one may be made liable in absence of any guilty state of mind. This happens in cases of mass destructions through pollution, gross negligence of the company resulting in widespread damage, much like in the Bhopal Gas tragedy.[3]

The development of the law relating to corporate criminal liability in India has not only been similar to that in

English law, but also greatly influenced by the English law. At one point of time, 'corporations' were viewed as a convenient shield to evade liability. However, under our the present penal structure, for an offence by the corporation, both the corporation and its officer can be made liable. The law on corporate criminal liability is however, not confined to the general criminal law in the penal code but it is, in fact, scattered over a plethora of statutes with specific provisions for the same. The instant example being in the case law no.3 cited further in the chapter where the liability is attached to the officers of the company under the Information Technology Act. The need for proper law relating to corporate criminal liability in a legal system, specially in the developing countries like India was observed by the Supreme Court in the following terms:

> In India, the need for industrial development has led to the establishment of a number of plants and factories by the domestic companies and undertakings as well as by Transnational Corporations. Many of these industries are engaged in hazardous or inherently dangerous activities which pose potential threat to life, health and safety of persons working in the factory, or residing in the surrounding areas. Though working of such factories and plants is regulated by a 614 number of laws of our country, there is no special legislation providing for compensation and damages to outsiders who may suffer on account of any industrial accident.

Hence under Indian law the liability of the company is essentially liability of the company only. Further, under Indian law as well as under the English law, a company is a creation of the law. It is not a human being but is an artificial person. On incorporation, the company acquires a separate legal entity distinct from and independent of its members. When a company is incorporated, all dealings are with the company and all persons behind the company are disregarded, however important they may be. Thus, a veil is drawn between the company and its members. Normally, the principle of corporate personality of a company is respected in most of the cases. The separate personality of the company is, however, a statutory privilege; it must be used for legal and legitimate business purposes only. Where a fraudulent, dishonest or improper use is made of the legal entity, the concerned individual will not be allowed to take shelter behind the corporate personality. The court will break through the corporate shell and apply the principle of "Lifting of the corporate veil". The court will look behind the corporate entity and take action as though no entity separate from the members existed. In other words, the benefit of separate legal entity will not be available and the court will presume the absence of such separate existence. The Companies Act, 1956 contains certain provisions,[4] which empower the courts to lift the veil to reach the persons who are in fact responsible for the culpable or wrongful act. The corporate veil can be lifted in the following cases:

a) Where the doctrine conflicts with the public policy.

b) Where corporate veil has been used for fraud or improper conduct.

c) Where the corporate facade is only an agency instrumentality.

d) For determining the real character of the company.

e) Where the veil has been used for evasion of taxes.

f) In quasi-criminal cases.

g) For investigating the ownership of the company.

h) For investigating the affairs of the company.

i) Where the company is used as a medium to avoid various welfare and labour legislations.

j) In case of economic offences.

k) Where the company is used for some illegal and improper purpose, etc.

> A company cannot be sent to jail, and if a fine is to be paid, it diminishes both the money available to pay the wages and salaries of all the remaining employees, and the profits available to pay all the existing shareholders. Thus, the effect of the only available punishment is deflected from the wrongdoer personally and distributed among all the innocent parties who supply the labour and the capital that keep the company solvent.

International Changes

The legislative changes towards checking the corporate crimes have already taken place in Australia, France (Penal Code of 1392), Netherlands (The Economic Offences Act, 1950 and Article 51 of Criminal Code), and Belgium (in 1934, Cour de Cassation recognised the punishment of a corporate body by making it a subject of Belgian Criminal Statute). Germany practices a sort of administrative sanction to deviant corporations and doesn't recognize criminal liability of corporations. The Canadian Federal Criminal Code 13 was amended as far back as in 1909 whereby a fine could be substituted for a sentence of imprisonment, made the corporate criminal liability possible. Section 718 of the Canadian Criminal Code imposes fine to corporate offenders and Section 720 provides special enforcement procedure for fines on corporations. The European Council in 1988 made a recommendation to the member states to carry out necessary amendments in their respective criminal statutes to ensure corporate liability, whereas, the United Kingdom follows the alter ego or identification approach to fix corporate liability in criminal cases.

In Australia, the Criminal Code is based upon the findings of a sub-committee of the Standing Committee of Attorneys-General from Federal, State and Territory Governments, which was formed to consider the development of a uniform criminal code for Australian jurisdictions. The Report favoured adoption of a species of corporate criminal liability which recognised independent corporate fault and would cast a substantially broader and "much more realistic net of responsibility over corporations" than the narrow liability under Tesco. The Committee's primary objective was to develop a liability scheme which "as nearly as possible, adapted personal criminal responsibility to fit the modern corporation". The Committee's alternative model of corporate criminal liability is now found in Pt 2.5 of the Criminal Code.

These provisions will be a bellwether for future developments in Australia in the field of corporate criminal responsibility and corporate governance generally. The structures of the provisions under Pt 2.5 of the Criminal Code are as follows. Section 12.1 provides that the Code applies, with necessary modifications, equally to bodies corporate as to natural persons, specifying that a "body corporate may be found guilty of any offence, including one punishable by imprisonment". Section 12.2 imposes vicarious liability upon the corporation for the physical elements (though not the mental element) of the offence when committed by any employee, agent or officer within the actual or apparent scope of employment. Under s.12.3 (1) of the Criminal Code, the requisite element of fault in an offence, characterised by, for example, intention, knowledge or recklessness, is established on the part of the body corporate itself, where the body corporate has "expressly, tacitly or impliedly authorised or permitted the commission of the offence".

The position of law regarding the same in USA is that the punishment of corporate crime is based on the doctrine of 'Respondent Superior', whereby the agent's conduct is imputed to the corporation. A corporation may be held criminally liable for the acts, omissions or failures of an agent acting within the scope of his employment.[5] The nature of incorporeal legal entities requires courts look to employees of the corporation as a means of imputing intent, or *mens rea,*[6] as well as the guilty act, or *actus reus,*[7] to the corporation. Courts hold a corporation vicariously liable for the acts of its employees if the individual: (i) acted within the scope and nature of his employment;[8] (ii) acted, at least in part, to benefit the corporation; and (iii) the act and intent can be imputed to the corporation.[9] In an effort to deter corporate crime more effectively, the US Sentencing Commission established a number of sentencing guidelines.[10] The Guidelines promulgate a wide range of sanctions available to the courts.

While corporate offenders are generally punished by way of fines in the United Kingdom, the US guidelines embrace radical remedial goals[11] Restitution orders are mandatory for all federal offences. To this end, the offender must make a payment to the victim of the crime, with the aim of "making the victim whole again for the harm caused". The guidelines also promulgate an appropriate punitive fine range for convicted organisations.

Indian Judicial Perspective qua Corporate Criminal Liability

The Iridium/Motorola Case[12] : Supreme Court

The Judgment of the Supreme Court in Iridium India Telecom Ltd. v. Motorola Inc.[13]

The question of punishing a corporation came up recently in the Supreme Court in a criminal case filed by Iridium India Telecom Ltd against Motorola Incorporated. The allegations were cheating and criminal conspiracy. The magistrate in Pune started proceedings against Motorola. It moved the Bombay High Court against the prosecution. The high court quashed the proceedings giving several reasons, one of them being that a corporation was incapable of committing the offence of cheating as it has no mind. According to the high court, although a company can be a victim of deception, it cannot be the perpetrator of deception. Only a natural person is capable of having a guilty mind to commit an offence.

The Hon'ble Supreme Court set aside the high court's finding and held that a corporate body can be prosecuted for cheating and conspiracy under the Indian Penal Code. The offences for which companies can be criminally prosecuted are not limited only to the specific provisions made in the Income Tax Act, the Essential Commodities Act, and the Prevention of Food Adulteration Act. Several other statutes also make a company liable for prosecution, conviction and sentence.

The Supreme Court allowed the appeal and set aside the order of the high court. The apex court allowed the prosecution to go on, stating that companies and corporate houses can no longer claim immunity from criminal prosecution on the ground that they are incapable of possessing the necessary mens rea for the commission of criminal offences.

In its ruling, the Supreme Court reiterated the legal position on two counts: (i) the scope of jurisdiction of the high court in quashing criminal proceedings under Section 482 of the Criminal Procedure Code; and (ii) the fact that companies can be prosecuted for offences involving *mens rea*. On the second count, the Supreme Court merely reiterated the principles laid down in the previous case of Standard Chartered Bank v. Directorate of Enforcement [(2005) 4 SCC 405].

The Supreme Court, however, did not have the opportunity to rule on certain other important aspects of the case, which relate to the liability of a company for misstatements or non-disclosures of information in memorandum issued in connection with the offering of securities, the same being the subject-matter of the prosecution that would continue now, after the Supreme Court giving a green signal to prosecution.

The facts of the Iridium Case were based on criminal complaint that pertained to a charge of cheating under section 420 read with section 120B (conspiracy) under the Indian Penal Code (I.P.C.). The allegation was that Motorala Inc., the respondent in the case and the primary contractor for the Iridium system/project, floated a private placement memorandum (PPM) to obtain funds/investments to finance the Iridium project. The project was "represented as being the world's first commercial system designed to provide global digital hand held telephone data ... and it was intended to be a wireless communication system through a constellation of 66 satellites in low orbit to provide digital service to mobile phones and other subscriber equipment locally." Several financial institutions invested in the project based on the information contained in the PPM. However, it was alleged that the representations were false and that the project turned out to be commercially unviable, resulting in significant loss to the investors.

A few interesting facts about the case were that the complaint was brought under the I.P.C. (being the general criminal law) and not under any specific corporate or securities legislation. It is understandable because the PPM did not pertain to a "public" offering of shares, and hence the relevant prospectus provisions (and concomitant liability issues therein) are not attracted. The transaction was in the nature of a private placement and hence governed contractually rather than as a matter of public securities laws.

Although the issuer had placed reliance on the extensive nature of risk factors and disclaimers in the PPM as a defence against criminal liability, the Supreme Court did not place much importance to cautionary language, at least at the stage of deciding whether to allow the prosecution to continue.

The Hon'ble Apex Court while allowing the appeal, held that:

a) There is much substance in the submission that virtually in all jurisdictions across the world governed by the rule of law, the companies and corporate houses can no longer claim immunity from criminal prosecution on the ground that they are incapable of possessing the necessary mens rea for the commission of criminal offences. The legal position in England and the United States has now crystallized to leave no manner of doubt that a corporation would be liable for crimes of intent.[14]

b) A corporation is virtually in the same position as any individual and may be convicted of common law as well as statutory offences including those requiring mens rea. The criminal liability of a corporation would arise when an offence is committed in relation to the business of the corporation by a person or body of persons in control of its affairs. In such circumstances, it would be necessary to ascertain that the degree and control of the person or body of persons is so intense that a corporation may be said to think and act through the person or the body of persons. The position of law on this issue in Canada is almost the same. *Mens rea* is attributed to corporations on the principle of the 'alter ego' of the company.[15]

c) A company/corporation cannot escape liability for a criminal offence, merely because the punishment prescribed is that of imprisonment and fine. The conclusion reached by the high court that the respondent could not have the necessary *mens rea* is clearly erroneous.[16]

d) A bare perusal of section 415 IPC would show that it can be conveniently divided into two parts. The first part makes it necessary that the deception by the accused of the person deceived, must be fraudulent or dishonest. Such deception must induce the person deceived to: either (a) deliver property to any person; or (b) consent that any person shall retain any property. The second part also requires that the accused must by deception intentionally induce the person deceived either to do or omit to do anything which he would not do or omit, if he was not so deceived.

Furthermore, such act or omission must cause or must be likely to cause damage or harm to that person in body, mind, reputation or property. Thus, it is evident that deception is a necessary ingredient for the offences of cheating under both parts of this section. The complainant, therefore, necessarily needs to prove that the inducement had been caused by the deception exercised by the accused. Such deception must necessarily produce the inducement to part with or deliver property, which the complainant would not have parted with or delivered, but for the inducement resulting from deception. The explanation to the section would clearly indicate that there must be no dishonest concealment of facts. In other words, non-disclosure of relevant information would also be treated as a mis-representation of facts leading to deception.[17]

e) It was necessary for the high court to examine the averments in the complaint in terms of s.415 IPC. The high court upon detailed examination of the 1992 PPM, the Stock Purchase Agreements and the 1995 PPM concluded that even if the averments made in the complaint are accepted on their face value, it would only disclose a civil dispute between the parties. According to the high court, respondent no. 1 did not keep the investors in dark about the Iridium System and gave them all necessary information in respect of various aspects of the system. In coming to the aforesaid conclusion, the high court observed that "a bare perusal of the complaint shows that there is no reference to the Stock Purchase Agreements of 1993 and 1994. In fact, these two important documents contain acknowledgments of the investors about their capability of evaluating the merits and risks of the purchase of the shares and their relying upon their own advisors." The high court, therefore, negated the submission that there has not been a complete and candid disclosure of the entire material which has resulted in the deception / inducement of the appellant to make huge investment in the Iridium. This conclusion reached by the high court did not take notice of the explanation to Section 415, which gives a statutory recognition to the legal principles established through various judicial pronouncements that misleading statements which withhold the vital facts for intentionally inducing a person to do or to omit to do something would amount to deception. Further, in case it is found that misleading statement has wrongfully caused damage to the person deceived it would amount to cheating.[18]

f) The appellants were entitled to an opportunity to prove the averments made in the complaint. They were entitled to establish that they had been deliberately induced into making huge investments on the basis of representations made by respondent no. 1 and its representatives, which representations subsequently turned out to be completely false and fraudulent. The appellants were entitled to an opportunity to establish that respondent no. 1 and its representatives were aware of the falsity of the representations at the time when they were made. The appellants gave elaborate details of the positive assertions made by respondent no. 1 which were allegedly false to its knowledge. It is also claimed by the appellants that respondent no. 1 and its representatives wilfully concealed facts which were material and ought to have been disclosed, but were intentionally withheld so as to deceive the appellant into advancing and expending a sum of Rs. 500 crores. Both the appellants and the respondents have much to say in support of their respective viewpoints. Which of the views is ultimately to be accepted, could only be decided when the parties have had the opportunities to place the entire materials before the court. The power to quash the proceedings at the initial stage have to be exercised sparingly with circumspection and in the rarest of the rare cases. The power is to be exercised *ex debito justitiae*. Such power can be exercised where a criminal proceeding is manifestly attended with malafide and have been instituted maliciously with ulterior motive. This inherent power ought not to be exercised to stifle a legitimate prosecution.[19]

g) In the circumstances of the instant case, the high court ought to have refrained from indulging in detailed analysis of very complicated commercial documents and reaching any definite conclusions. The high court clearly exceeded its jurisdiction in quashing the criminal proceeding in the peculiar facts and circumstances of the case. The high court noticed that while exercising jurisdiction under Section 482 CrPC, "the complaint in its entirety will have to be examined on the basis of the allegations made therein. But the high court has no authority or jurisdiction to go into the matter or examine its correctness. The allegations in the complaint will have to be accepted on the face of it and the truth or falsity cannot be entered into by the court at this stage." Having said so, the high court proceeded to do exactly the opposite. The judgment of the high court is set aside. [Para 45 and 46] [641-G-H; 642-A-C]

The Hon'ble Supreme Court referred many cases while adjudicating the corporate liability for crimes in the Iridium case discussed above. Excerpts of some of them are consolidated herein below for better understanding of the law since its inception. **Country** : United States of America, Year : 1909, Citation : [53 L Ed 613]**The United States Supreme Court in** ***New York Central & Hudson River Railroad Co. Vs. United States***, **stated the principle thus:-**"*It is true that there are some crimes which, in their nature, cannot be committed by corporations. But there is a large class of offences, of which rebating under the federal statutes is one, wherein the crime consists in purposely doing the things prohibited by statute. In that class of crimes we see no good reason why corporations may not be held responsible for and charged with the knowledge and purposes of their agents, acting within the authority conferred upon them. If it were not so, many offences might go unpunished and acts be committed in violation of law where, as in the present case, the statute requires all persons, corporate or private, to refrain from certain practices, forbidden in the interest of public policy.* * * *We see no valid objection in law, and every reason in public policy, why the corporation, which profits by the transaction, and can only act through its agents and officers, shall be held punishable by fine because of the knowledge and intent of its agents to whom it has entrusted authority to act in the subject-matter of making and fixing rates of transportation, and whose knowledge and purposes may well be attributed to the corporation for which the agents act. While the law should have regard to the rights of all, and to those of corporations no less than to those of individuals, it cannot shut its eyes to the fact that the great majority of business transactions in modern times are conducted through these bodies, and particularly that inter-State commerce is almost entirely in their hands, and to give them immunity from all punishment because of the old and exploded doctrine that a corporation cannot commit a crime would virtually take away the only means of effectually controlling the subject-matter and correcting the abuses aimed at.*"**The aforesaid sentiment is**

reiterated in the 19 American Jurisprudence 2d para 1434 **in the following words:-** *"Lord Holt is reported to have said (Anonymous, 12 Mod 559, 88 Eng Reprint 1164) that 'a corporation is not indictable, but the particular members of it are'. On the strength of this statement it was said by the early writers that a corporation is not indictable at common law, and this view was taken by the courts in some of the earlier cases. The broad general rule is now well established, however, that a corporation may becriminally liable. This rule applies as well to acts of misfeasance as to those of nonfeasance, and it is immaterial that the Act constituting the offence was ultra vires. It has been held that a de facto corporation may be held criminally liable. As in case of torts the general rule prevails that a corporation may be criminally liable for the acts of an officer or agent, assumed to be done by him when exercising authorized powers, and without proof that his act was expressly authorized or approved by the corporation. A specific prohibition made by the corporation to its agents against violation of the law is no defence. The rule has been laid down, however, that corporations are liable, civilly or criminally, only for the acts of their agents who are authorized to act for them in the particular matter out of which the unlawful conduct with which they are charged grows or in thebusiness to which it relates."* **Again in** 19 Corpus Juris Secundum, para 1363 **it has been observed as under:-** *"A corporation may be criminally liable for crimes which involve a specific element of intent as well for those which do not, and, although some crimes require such a personal, malicious intent, that a corporation is considered incapable of committing them, nevertheless, under the proper circumstances the criminal intent of its agent may be imputed to it so as to render it liable, the requisites of such imputation being essentially the same as those required to impute malice to corporations in civil actions."* Case: Director of Public Prosecutions Vs. Kent and Sussex Contractors Ltd. **observations made by the** MacNaghten, J. ; Citation : 1944 1 All ER 119 *"A body corporate is a 'person' to whom, amongst the various attributes it may have, there should be imputed the attribute of a mind capable of knowing and forming an intention — indeed* *it is much too late in the day to suggest the contrary. It can only know or form an intention through its human agents, but circumstances may be such that the knowledge of the agent must be imputed to the body corporate. Counsel for the respondents says that, although a body corporate may be capable of having an intention, it is not capable of having a criminal intention. In this particular case the intention was the intention to deceive. If, as in this case, the responsible agent of a body corporate puts forward a document knowing it to be false and intending that it should deceive, I apprehend, according to the authorities that Viscount Caldecote, L.C.J., has cited, his knowledge and intention must be imputed to the body corporate."* The principle has been reiterated by Lord Denning in the case of H.L.Bolton (Engg.) Co. Ltd. Vs. T.J.Graham & Sons (1956 3 All ER 624) in the following words:- *"A company may in many ways be likened to a human body. They have a brain and a nerve centre which controls what they do. They also have hands which hold the tools and act in accordance with directions from the centre. Some of the people in the company are mere servants and agents who are nothing more than hands to do the work and cannot be said to represent the mind or will. Others are directors and managers who represent the directing mind and will of the company, and control what they do. The state of mind of these managers is the state of mind of the company and is treated by the law as such. So you will find that in cases where the law requires personal fault as a condition of liability in tort, the fault of the manager will be the personal fault of the company. That is made clear in Lord Haldane's speech in Lennard's Carrying Co. Ltd. Vs. Asiatic Petroleum Co. Ltd. (AC at pp. 713, 714). So also in the criminal law, in cases where the law requires a guilty mind as a condition of a criminal offence, the guilty mind of the directors or the managers will render the company themselves guilty."* The aforesaid principle has been firmly established in England since the decision of House of Lords in Tesco Supermarkets Ltd. Vs. Nattrass (1971 All ER 127). In stating the principle of corporate liability for criminal offences, Lord Reid made the following statement of law:- *"I must start by considering the nature of the personality which by a fiction the law attributes to a corporation. A living person has a mind which can have knowledge or intention or be negligent and he has hands to carry out his intentions. A corporation has none of these; it must act through living persons, though not always one or the same person. Then the person who acts is not speaking or acting for the company. He is acting as the company and his mind which directs his acts is the mind of the company. There is no question of the company being vicariously liable. He is not acting as a servant, representative, agent or delegate. He is an embodiment of the company or, one could say, he hears and speaks through the persona of the company, within his appropriate sphere, and his mind is the mind of the company. If it is guilty mind then that guilt is the guilt of the company. It must be a question of law whether, once the facts have been ascertained, a person in doing particular things is to be regarded as the company or merely as the company's servant or agent. In that case any liability of the company can only be a statutory or vicarious liability."*

The Supreme Court discussing the above legal position further held:

> "From the above it becomes evident that a corporation is virtually in the same position as any individual and may be convicted of common law as well as statutory offences including those requiring mens rea. The criminal liability of a corporation would arise when an offence is committed in relation to the business of the corporation by a person or body of persons in control of its affairs. In such circumstances, it would be necessary to ascertain that the degree and control of the person or body of persons is so intense that a corporation may be said to think and act through the person or the body of persons. The position of law on this issue in Canada is almost the same. Mens rea is attributed to corporations on the principle of 'alter ego' of the company."

The apex court termed the conclusion of the high court that the respondent could not have the necessary *mens rea*, as erroneous. The apex court also affirmed the judgment in the case of standard chartered and held that it leaves no manner of doubt that a company / corporation cannot escape liability for a criminal offence, merely because the punishment prescribed is that of imprisonment and fine.

The most important judgment on the issue of corporate liability has been rendered by the Supreme Court Constitution Bench in the matter titled as Standard Chartered Bank Vs. Directorate of Enforcement[20] after considering the entire body of case law of this country and other jurisdictions as well.

It was held in that case:

> There is no dispute that a company is liable to be prosecuted and punished for criminal offences. Although there are earlier authorities to the effect that corporations cannot commit a crime, the generally accepted modern rule is that except for such crimes as a corporation is held incapable of committing by reason of the fact that they involve personal malicious intent, a corporation may be subject to indictment or other criminal process, although the criminal act is committed through its agents.

Pertinent observations of the apex court in that case, which has become the law governing the corporate criminal liability, have been reproduced herein below.

> 27. In the case of Penal Code offences, for example under Section 420 of the Indian Penal Code, for cheating and dishonestly inducing delivery of property, the punishment prescribed is imprisonment of either description for a term which may extend to seven years and shall also be liable to fine; and for the offence under Section 417, that is, simple cheating, the punishment prescribed is imprisonment of either description for a term which may extend to one year or with

fine or with both. If the appellants' plea is accepted then for the offence under Section 417 IPC, which is an offence of minor nature, a company could be prosecuted and punished with fine whereas for the offence under Section 420, which is an aggravated form of cheating by which the victim is dishonestly induced to deliver property, the company cannot be prosecuted as there is a mandatory sentence of imprisonment.

28. So also there are several other offences in the Indian Penal Code which describe offences of serious nature whereunder a corporate body also may be found guilty, and the punishment prescribed is mandatory custodial sentence. There are a series of other offences under various statutes where the accused are also liable to be punished with custodial sentence and fine.

30. As the company cannot be sentenced to imprisonment, the court has to resort to punishment of imposition of fine which is also a prescribed punishment. As per the scheme of various enactments and also the Indian Penal Code, mandatory custodial sentence is prescribed for graver offences. If the appellants' plea is accepted, no company or corporate bodies could be prosecuted for the graver offences whereas they could be prosecuted for minor offences as the sentence prescribed therein is custodial sentence or fine.

31. As the company cannot be sentenced to imprisonment, the court cannot impose that punishment, but when imprisonment and fine is the prescribed punishment the court can impose the punishment of fine which could be enforced against the company. Such a discretion is to be read into the section so far as the juristic person is concerned. Of course, the court cannot exercise the same discretion as regards a natural person. Then the court would not be passing the sentence in accordance with law. As regards company, the court can always impose a sentence of fine and the sentence of imprisonment can be ignored as it is impossible to be carried out in respect of a company. This appears to be the intention of the legislature and we find no difficulty in construing the statute in such a way. We do not think that there is a blanket immunity for any

> company from any prosecution for serious offences merely because the prosecution would ultimately entail a sentence of mandatory imprisonment. The corporate bodies, such as a firm or company undertake a series of activities that affect the life, liberty and property of the citizens. Large-scale financial irregularities are done by various corporations. The corporate vehicle now occupies such a large portion of the industrial, commercial and sociological sectors that amenability of the corporation to a criminal law is essential to have a peaceful society with stable economy.
>
> 32. We hold that there is no immunity to the companies from prosecution merely because the prosecution is in respect of offences for which the punishment prescribed is mandatory imprisonment (sic and fine). We overrule the views expressed by the majority in Velliappa Textiles[1] on this point and answer the reference accordingly. Various other contentions have been urged in all appeals, including this appeal, they be posted for hearing before an appropriate Bench.

I have discussed the theories of corporate criminal liability in the previous chapter. I have collected and referred some important case laws here, to have a better understanding of corporate criminal liability.

Case Law No. 1

The Supreme Court of India in Aneeta Hada vs M/S Godfather Travels & Tours 21 decided on 8 May, 2008, discussed the extent of corporate criminal liability in case of a company. The issue involved in the matter was of liability of a company in the case of dishonour of a cheque. It was held by Justice S.B. Sinha:

> . . . The question as to whether a company can be proceeded against when a mandatory imprisonment is prescribed in law came up for consideration before a Constitution Bench of this Court in *Standard Chartered Bank and Others v. Directorate of Enforcement and Others* [(2005) 4 SCC 530] wherein this

Court upon considering a large number of decisions as also the principle "lex non cogit ad impossibilia" opined:

30. As the company cannot be sentenced to imprisonment, the court has to resort to punishment of imposition of fine which is also a prescribed punishment. As per the scheme of various enactments and also the Indian Penal Code, mandatory custodial sentence is prescribed for graver offences. If the appellants' plea is accepted, no company or corporate bodies could be prosecuted for the graver offences whereas they could be prosecuted for minor offences as the sentence prescribed therein is custodial sentence or fine. We do not think that the intention of the legislature is to give complete immunity from prosecution to the corporate bodies for these grave offences.

The offences mentioned under Section 56(1) of the FERA Act, 1973, namely, those under Section 13; clause (a) of sub-section (1) of Section 18; Section 18-A; clause (a) of sub-section (1) of Section 19; sub-section (2) of Section 44, for which the minimum sentence of six months' imprisonment is prescribed, are serious offences and if committed would have serious financial consequences affecting the economy of the country. All those offences could be committed by company or corporate bodies. We do not think that the legislative intent is not to prosecute the companies for these serious offences, if these offences involve the amount or value of more than Rs. one lakh, and that they could be prosecuted only when the offences involve an amount or value less than Rs. one lakh. (Emphasis supplied)

31. As the company cannot be sentenced to imprisonment, the court cannot impose that punishment, but when imprisonment and fine is the prescribed punishment the court can impose the punishment of fine which could be enforced against the company. Such a discretion is to be read into the section so far as the juristic person is concerned. Of course, the court cannot exercise the same discretion as regards a natural person. Then the court would not be passing the sentence in accordance with law. As regards company, the court can always impose a sentence of fine and the sentence of imprisonment can be ignored as it is impossible to be carried out in respect of a company. This appears to be the intention of the legislature

> and we find no difficulty in construing the statute in such a way. We do not think that there is a blanket immunity for any company from any prosecution for serious offences merely because the prosecution would ultimately entail a sentence of mandatory imprisonment. The corporate bodies, such as a firm or company undertake a series of activities that affect the life, liberty and property of the citizens. Large-scale financial irregularities are done by various corporations. The corporate vehicle now occupies such a large portion of the industrial, commercial and sociological sectors that amenability of the corporation to a criminal law is essential to have a peaceful society with stable economy.

In the context of the provisions of the Income Tax Act, recently a Division Bench of this Court in *Madhumilan Syntex Ltd. & Ors. v. Union of India & Anr.* [AIR 2007 SC 1481], held:

> 23. From the above provisions, it is clear that wherever a Company is required to deduct tax at source and to pay it to the account of the Central Government, failure on the part of the Company in deducting or in paying such amount is an offence under the Act and has been made punishable. It, therefore, cannot be said that the prosecution against a Company or its Directors in default of deducting or paying tax is not envisaged by the Act.
>
> 24. It is no doubt true that Company is not a natural person but 'legal' or 'juristic' person. That, however, does not mean that Company is not liable to prosecution under the Act. 'Corporate criminal liability' is not unknown to law. The law is well settled on the point and it is not necessary to discuss it in detail.

20. In *Sabitha Ramamurthy and Anr. v. R.B.S. Channabasavaradhya* [2006 (9) SCALE 212], this court held that though a person was not personally liable for the offences committed by the company, however, he would only be liable vicariously for the acts of company in terms of Section 141 of the Act only if the requisite averments, are made in the complaint petition.

21. In *S.V. Muzumdar and Ors. v. Gujarat State Fertilizer Co. Ltd. and Anr.* (2005) 4 SCC 173, this Court explicitly laid down the following categories of persons who are covered under Section 141 of the act: (1) The company who committed the offence. (2) Everyone who was in charge of and was responsible for the business of the company. (3) Any other person who is a director or a manager or a secretary or officer of the company with whose connivance or due to whose neglect the company has committed the offence.

In *Municipal Corporation of Delhi v. Ram Kishan Rohtagi and Ors.* [(1983) 1 SCC 1], the Respondent No. 1 was the manager and respondents No. 2 to 5 were directors of X company. Respondents were charged for offences under Sections 7 and 16 of the Prevention of Food Adulteration Act, 1954 and Section 482 of Criminal Procedure Code, 1973 as the toffees manufactured by X company was found to be not conforming to the standards prescribed for toffees. On appeal, the high court quashed the proceedings against respondents. It was held by this court that:

> So far as the Manager is concerned, we are satisfied that from the very nature of his duties it can be safely inferred that he would undoubtedly be vicariously liable for the offence; vicarious liability being an incident of an offence under the Act. So far as the Directors are concerned, there is not even a whisper nor a shred of evidence nor anything to show, apart from the presumption drawn by the complainant, that there is any act committed by the Directors from which a reasonable inference can be drawn that they could also be vicariously liable.

However, as regards the manager of the company, the court held that since he could not fall in the same category as the directors, and as he was directly incharge of the affairs of the company, he should be held to be liable.

Assistant Commissioner, Assessment-II Bangalore & Ors vs. Velliappa Textiles Ltd & Anr. (2003) 11 SCC 405:

> . . . In this case (supra), by a majority decision it was held that the company cannot be prosecuted for offences which require imposition of a mandatory term of imprisonment coupled with fine. It was further held that where punishment provided is imprisonment and fine, the court cannot impose only a fine. In Velliappa Textiles, prosecution was launched against the respondent, a private limited company, for the offences punishable under Sections 276-C, 277 and 278 read with Section 278-B of the Income Tax Act. Under Section 276-C and 277 of the Income Tax Act, the substantive sentence provided is the sentence of imprisonment and fine. Speaking for the majority, one of us (Srikrishna, J.) held that the first respondent company cannot be prosecuted for offences under Section 276-C, 277 and 278 read with Section 278-B since each of these sections requires the imposition of a mandatory term of imprisonment coupled with a fine and leaves no choice to the court to impose only a fine. The majority was of the view that the legislative mandate is to prohibit the courts from deviating from the minimum mandatory punishment prescribed by the Statute and that while interpreting a penal statute, if more than one view is possible, the court is obliged to lean in favour of the construction which exempts a citizen from penalty than the one which imposes the penalty. Following the decision in *State of Maharashtra vs. Jugamander Lal AIR 1966 SC 940*, it was held that the expression used is "imprisonment and fine" and the court is bound to award sentence of imprisonment as well as fine and that there is no discretion on the part of the court to impose only a fine and that the court cannot interpret the statutory provisions in a way so as to supply a lacuna in a statute.

A full Bench of the Delhi High Court in *Delhi Municiaplity vs. J.B. Bottling Company 1975 Crl. L.J. 1148* considered a similar question. The respondent-company was found guilty under Section 7 read with Section 16 of the Prevention of Food Adulteration Act, and was fined Rs. 5,000. The respondent-company filed an appeal and contended that for the offence under Section 16 of the Prevention of Food Adulteration Act, the minimum period of six months' imprisonment is prescribed and the company is immune from prosecution as the sentence contemplated under law cannot be imposed on it. The court held that:

> The office of the judges is always to make construction as shall suppress the mischief and advance the remedy and therefore it will stay its hand in passing the sentence which will be impossible to execute but pass only such sentence which can be executed, namely, fine. The proviso to Section 16 applies only to the three classes of offences mentioned therein and as compared to the rest of the offences contemplated by the Act are of less serious nature and if indictment of the company is confined to only those offences which are covered by the proviso, then not only the intention of the legislature is defeated, but the provisions of Section 16(1-D) and Section 18 are also to that extent rendered nugatory, insofar as the offences are committed by the companies.

In *Oswal Vanaspati & Allied Industries vs. State of Uttar Pradesh (1993) 1 Comp. L.J. 172 (All.)*, the appellant-company sought to quash the complaint filed against it by the food inspector under various sections of the Act alleging that the company cannot be prosecuted for an offence under Section 16 of the Act as the sentence of imprisonment provided under that section after its amendment by the Prevention of Food Adulteration (Amendment) Act No. 34 of 1976 which is mandatory cannot be awarded to it. In paragraph 7, the Full Bench of the Allahabad High Court held as follows:

> A company being a juristic person cannot obviously be sentenced to imprisonment as it cannot suffer imprisonment. The question that requires determination is whether a sentence of fine alone can be imposed on it under Section 16 of the Act or whether such a sentence would be illegal and hence cannot be awarded to it.

It is settled law that sentence or punishment must follow conviction; and if only corporal punishment is prescribed, a company which is a juristic person cannot be prosecuted as it cannot be punished. If, however, both sentence of imprisonment and fine is prescribed for natural persons and juristic persons jointly, then, though the sentence of imprisonment cannot be awarded to a company, the sentence of fine can be imposed on it. Thus it cannot be held that in such a case the entire sentence prescribed cannot be awarded to a company as a part of the sentence, namely, that of fine can be awarded to it. Legal sentence is the sentence prescribed by law. A sentence which is in excess of the sentence prescribed is always illegal; but a sentence which is less than the sentence prescribed may not in all cases be illegal.

It is also appropriate to make reference to a decision of the United States Supreme Court. The judgment was rendered in *United States vs. Union Supply Company 54 Law. Ed. 87* by Justice Holmes. There was an indictment of a corporation for wilfully violating the sixth section of the Act of Congress of 1902 and any person who wilfully violates any of the provisions of this Section shall, for each such offence, be liable to be punished with fine not less than $ 50 and not exceeding $ 500, and imprisonment for not less than 30 days, nor more than six months. It is interesting to note that for the offence under Section 5, the court had discretionary power to punish by either fine or imprisonment, whereas under Section 6, both punishments were to be imposed in all cases. The plea of the company was rejected and it was held:

> It seems to us that a reasonable interpretation of the words used does not lead to such a result. If we compare Section 5, the application of one of the penalties rather than of both is made to depend, not on the character of the defendant, but on the discretion of the Judge; yet, there, corporations are mentioned in terms. And if we free our minds from the notion that criminal statutes must be construed by some artificial and

> conventional rule, the natural inference, when a statute prescribes two independent penalties, is that it means to inflict them so far as it can, and that, if one of them is impossible, it does not mean, on that account, to let the defendant escape.

A passage in Craies on Statue Law 7th Edn. reads to the following effect:

> The distinction between a strict and a liberal construction has almost disappeared with regard to all classes of statutes, so that all statutes, whether penal or not, are now construed by substantially the same rules. 'All modern Acts are framed with regard to equitable as well as legal principles.' "A hundred years ago", said the court in Lyons' case, "statutes were required to be perfectly precise and resort was not had to a reasonable construction of the Act, and thereby criminals were often allowed to escape. This is not the present mode of construing Acts of Parliament. They are construed now with reference to the true meaning and real intention of the legislature.

At page 532 of the same book, the observations of Sedgwick are quoted as under:

> The more correct version of the doctrine appears to be that statutes of this class are to be fairly construed and faithfully applied according to the intent of the legislature without unwarrantable severity on the one hand or unjustifiable lenity on the other, in cases of doubt the courts inclining to mercy.

Case Law No. 2

In another significant judgment by the Supreme Court of India in *Anz Grindlays Bank Limited & Ors., ... vs Directorate Of Enforcement* by Justice K Balakrishnan,[22] the question that arose for consideration was whether a company or a corporate body could be prosecuted for offences for which the sentence of imprisonment is a mandatory punishment. It was held in that judgment:

As the company cannot be sentenced to imprisonment, the court cannot impose that punishment, but when imprisonment and fine is the prescribed punishment the court can impose the punishment of fine which could be enforced against the company. Such a discretion is to be read into the Section so far as the juristic person is concerned. Of course, the court cannot exercise the same discretion as regards a natural person. Then the court would not be passing the sentence in accordance with law. As regards company, the court can always impose a sentence of fine and the sentence of imprisonment can be ignored as it is impossible to be carried out in respect of a company. This appears to be the intention of the legislature and we find no difficulty in construing the statute in such a way. We do not think that there is a blanket immunity for any company from any prosecution for serious offences merely because the prosecution would ultimately entail a sentence of mandatory imprisonment. The corporate bodies, such as a firm or company undertake series of activities that affect the life, liberty and property of the citizens. Large scale financial irregularities are done by various corporations. The corporate vehicle now occupies such a large portion of the industrial, commercial and sociological sectors that amenability of the corporation to a criminal law is essential to have a peaceful society with stable economy. We hold that there is no immunity to the companies from prosecution merely because the prosecution is in respect of offences for which the punishment prescribed is mandatory imprisonment. We overrule the views expressed by the majority in Velliappa Textiles on this point and answer the reference accordingly.

Case Law No. 3

In an interesting case of deemed criminal liability which arose out of the infamous MMS of school children from New Delhi, came up for consideration before the Delhi High Court, which was decided by Justice S. Muralidhar in *Avnish Bajaj vs State on 29 May, 2008*. The facts of the case were, that an internet website carried a listing which offered for sale a video clip, shot on a mobile phone, of two children of a school in Delhi indulging in an explicitly sexual act. The petitioner, who was the Managing Director (MD) of the company, i.e., Bazee India Private Limited (BIPL) that owned the website at the relevant point in time, asked the Hon'ble High Court to annul his criminal prosecution for the offences of making available for sale and causing to be published an obscene product within the meaning of Section 292 Indian Penal Code (IPC) and Section 67 of the Information Technology Act 2000 (IT Act).

This petition under Section 482 of the Code of Criminal Procedure 1973 ('CrPC') also raised questions concerning the criminal liability of directors for the offences attributable to a company, both under the IPC as well as the IT Act, particularly when such company is not arraigned as an accused.

The Hon'ble Court while appreciating that the regulation of pornography on the internet has become a serious challenge to the Governments and the Legislatures primarily on account of the nature of medium. The Hon'ble Court quoted that "controlling pornography on the internet is problematic because we may not know from whom or from where the material originates, how many people are receiving the information, or if the material is crossing international boundaries." [See Robyn Forman Pollack, "*Creating the Standards of a Global Community: Regulating Pornography on the Internet-an International Concern*" *10 Temple International and Comparative Law Journal*, (Fall, 1996) 467].

The Hon'ble Judge in the judgment also mentioned that "the main concern of the legislators and parents in relation to the internet is child pornography, rather than other forms of sexually explicit content. This has been the case ever since paedophiles started to use the internet for circulating pornographic materials related to children." [See Yaman Akdeniz, "Cyber Rights, Protection and Markets: Article Governing Pornography and Child Pornography on the Internet: The UK Approach" 32

University of West Los Angeles Law Review 247 (2001)]. Akdeniz points out that although in some countries there are arguments against proscription of pornography based on freedom of speech concerns, "there is general consensus that the line should be drawn with child pornography." These factors need to be borne in mind while examining the irreversible harm that can be caused by making available on the internet sexually explicit material that answers the description of child pornography.

The court held that upon reading the chargesheet as a whole, the prima-facie offence under sections 292 (1) (a) & (d) is made out against the company BIPL in respect of listing the video clip containing obscene content. Although the petitioner who was the Managing Director of BIPL was exonerated from the charges under Section 292 of the IPC, since the IPC does not recognized the concept an automatic criminal liability attaching to the director where the company is an accused. The Court discharged the Managing Director as far as the offences under sections 292 & 294 of the IPC are concerned, holding that the charge sheet does not make out even a prima facie case against him and only seeks to implicate him in his designation as MD of BIPL and not in his individual capacity.

The court discussed various decisions of the Supreme Court and held that a prima facie case under Section 67 read with Section 85 of the Information Technology Act is made out against the petitioner, since the law recognises the deemed criminal liability of the directors even where the Company is not arraigned as an accused.

What can be seen is that the concept of corporate criminal liability is evolving more through the judicial analysis than the legislative changes in the law. However, whichever way it may be, the clarity is welcome as the concept requires authentic principles to be formulated, in the present scene where the number of corporate and business houses are growing as never before.

Sections 292(2) (a) and 292 (2) (d) of the Indian Penal Code are reproduced herein for understanding:

Section 292 (2) "Whoever:

(a) Sells, lets to hire, distributes, publicly exhibits or in any manner puts into circulation, or for purposes of sale, hire, distribution, public exhibition or circulation, makes, produces or has in his possession any obscene book, pamphlet, paper, drawing, painting, representation or figure or any other obscene object whatsoever, or

....

(d) Advertise or makes known by any means whatsoever that any person is engaged or is ready to engage in any act which is an offence under this section, or that any such obscene object can be procured from or through any person, or

..........................."

The Sections 67 & 85 of the IT Act are also reproduced below to understand the scope of the same:

"Section 67 in The Information Technology Act, 2000

67. *Publishing of information which is obscene in electronic form.* Whoever publishes or transmits or causes to be published in the electronic form, any material which is lascivious or appeals to the prurient interest or if its effect is such as to tend t deprave and corrupt persons who are likely, having regard to all relevant circumstances, to read, see or hear the matter contained or embodied in it, shall be punished on first conviction with imprisonment of either description for a term which may exte d to five years and with fine which may extend to one lakh rupees and in the event of a second or subsequent conviction with imprisonment of either description for a term which may extend to ten years and also with fine which may extend to two lakh rupees."

"85. *Offences by companies.*

(1) Where a person committing a contravention of any of the provisions of this Act or of any rule, direction or order made thereunder is a company, every person who, at the time the contravention was committed, was in charge of and was responsible to, the company for the conduct of business of the company as well as the company, shall be guilty of the contravention and shall be liable to be proceeded against and punished accordingly: Provided that nothing contained in this sub- section shall render any such person liable to punishment if he proves that the contravention took place without his knowledge or that he exercised all due diligence to prevent such contravention.

(2) Notwithstanding anything contained in sub- section (1), where a contravention of any of the provisions of this Act or of any rule, direction or order made thereunder has been committed by a company and it is proved that the contravention has taken pla e with the consent or connivance of, or is attributable to any neglect on the part of, any director, manager, secretary or other officer of the company, such director, manager, secretary or other officer shall also be deemed to be guilty of the contraven ion and shall be liable to be proceeded against and punished accordingly. *Explanation*.- For the purposes of this section,-

(i) " company" means any body corporate and includes a firm or other association of individuals; and

(ii) " director", in relation to a firm, means a partner in the firm."

Notes and References

1. Actus reus connotes those result of human conduct which is forbidden by law and hence constitutes of human action; result of conduct and act prohibited by law. On other hand mens rea is generally taken as blame worthy mental condition: Russell, W.O., *Russell on Crime*, pp.17-51 (J.W.C. Turner Ed., New Delhi; Universal Law Publishing Pvt., 2001).
2. A. Ashworth, *Principles of Criminal Law*, pp. 79-81 (Oxford: Clarendon Press, 1991) cited by Fisse, *Reconstructing Corporate Criminal Law: Deterrence, Retribution, Fault, and Sanctions*, 56 S. Cal. L. Rev. 1141
3. 5 Assn. of Victims of Uphaar Tragedy v. UOI, 104(2003)DLT234
4. Sections 45, 147, 212, 239, 242 and 247
5. N.Y. Cent. & Hudson River R.R. Co. v. United States, 212 U.S. 481, 491-95 (1909) (finding corporation liable because it acts only through its agents or employees whose knowledge and purpose may be attributed to the corporation); see also United States v. Photogrammetric Data Serv., 259 F.3d 229, 242 (4th Cir. 2001) (holding that a corporation can act only through the conduct of its agents). For an in-depth discussion of the development of corporate criminal liability before N.Y. Cent., see generally Shaun P. Martin, Intracorporate Conspiracies, 50 *STAN. L. REV.* 399, 406 (1998).
6. See N.Y. Cent., 212 U.S. at 493 ("[A] corporation may be liable criminally for certain offenses of which a specific intent may be a necessary element." (quoting *Telegram Newspaper Co. v. Commonwealth, 52 N.E. 445, 446* (Mass.1899))); see also *United States v. Sain, 141 F.3d 463, 475* (3d Cir. 1998) (noting if agent of corporation conspires with another, corporation may take on mental state of agent through doctrine of respondeat superior and be criminally liable for conspiracy); *United States v. Sun-Diamond Growers, 964 F. Supp. 486, 490* (D.D.C. 1997) (noting many circuits have required government to "establish, beyond a reasonable doubt, that the agent acted within the scope of his employment with the intent to benefit the corporation" in order to hold corporation liable for acts of its employees).
7. See N.Y. Cent., 212 U.S. at 494 (holding corporation can be held responsible for illegal act of authorized employee of company). Actus reus, or the "guilty act," is defined as "[a] wrongful deed that

comprises the physical components of a crime and that generally must be coupled with mens rea to establish criminal liability; a forbidden act." Black's Law Dictionary (8th ed. 2004).

8. *United States v. One Parcel of Land, 965 F.2d 311, 316* (7th Cir. 1992) (stating agent's knowledge of illegal act may be imputed to corporation if agent was "acting as authorized and motivated at least in part by an intent to benefit the corporation" (citing *Zero v. United States, 459 U.S. 991* (1982))).
9. In re Hellenic, Inc., 252 F.3d 391, 395 (5th Cir. 2001) ("An agent's knowledge is imputed to the corporation where the agent is acting within the scope of his authority and where the knowledge relates to matters within the scope of that authority.").
10. FN58. *United States Sentencing Commission Guidelines Manual* (1991), Chap.8 (hereinafter "USSG"). The guidelines were in fact initially for individuals but were expanded to encompass corporations.
11. FN60. R.S. Gruner, "Beyond Fines :Innovative Corporate Sentences Under Federal Sentencing Guidelines" (1993) 71 *Washington University Law Review* 261 at 267.)
12. Criminal Appeal No. 688 of 2005, dated 20.10.2010 by Hon'ble Supreme Court of India
13. Analysis by M.J. Antony, dt 20.10.10, *Business Standard.*
14. [Para 35] [628-C-D].
15. [Para 38] [633-A-C].
16. [Para 40] [635-H; 636-A].
17. [Para 42] [636-F-H; 637-A-B].
18. [Paras 42, 44] [637-C-D; 638-E-H; 639-A-B].
19. [Para 44] [640-H; 641-A-E].
20. [(2005) 4 SCC 405.
21. Appeal (crl.) 838 of 2008.
22. Appeal (civil) 1748 of 1999.

4

Family Company Frauds

In countries like India where the sentiments of the people are woven together with social and family sentiments, it is very common to have companies owned virtually by the families. Since the business, the efforts and endeavour of different members of the family is collectively responsible to earn profits, in such cases usually the father is the managing director and the major shareholder, while the sons or daughters are the other directors and shareholders.

Mostly family owned businesses run on this typical structure. Over the past two decades, there has been a strong growth towards corporatization of proprietorship firms, and with this shift the obvious benefits have been availed by the business houses. But alongwith it, have also increased the risks of fraud being committed in such companies. Obviously, the company law doesn't recognize any distinction between a business company being held and run through different individuals and a company being completely owned and run by a family.

The lack of such distinction has created few problems over the years. In as much as the change in directorships or shareholdings is concerned, there have been innumerable instances which have been referred to the company law board and to the high courts to determine the allegation of fraud played by one member on the other.

Before we move forward towards the topic, I would suggest a reading of the illustration below to have an understanding of the typical family company structure. This is based upon a true case based out of New Delhi, India.

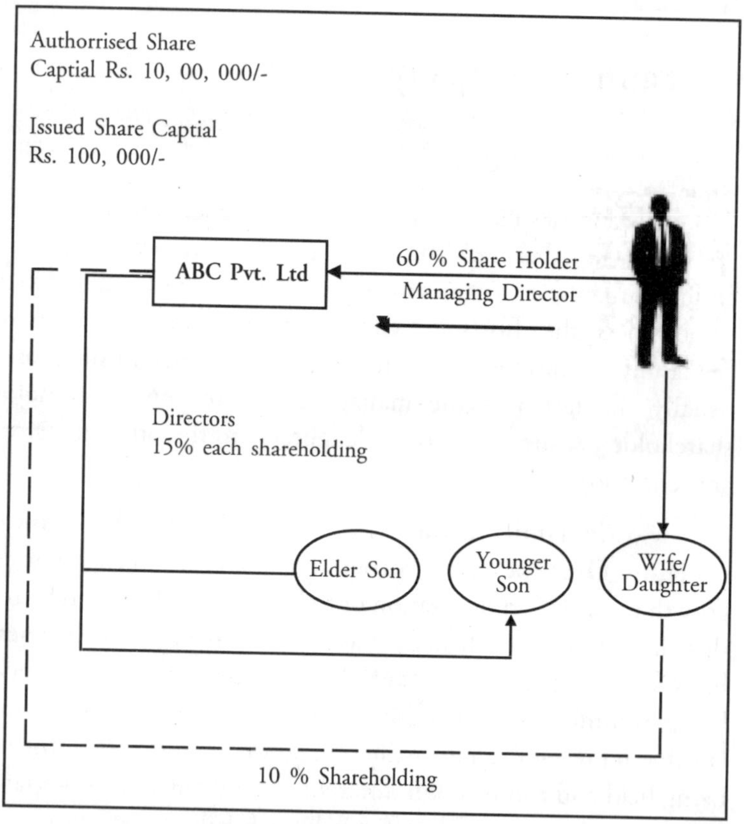

Illustration: Typical Family Company Structure

Now in the above illustration, a typical family company structure is described. ABC Pvt. Ltd. is a private limited company which has three directors, including one managing director being the father and two directors being the sons, who also are taking part in the running of the family business. While the majority stake is being held by the father, both the sons and the wife (or the daughter) also hold 15 per cent and 10% shares respectively.

Now to understand the modus of how the crime (or financial manipulations) could be committed within this company, we'll have to take the illustration a bit further. And by doing this, I only wish to take you through the facts of the real life cases which I have dealt with, being a legal expert on financial crimes. Sadly, these incidents also bring out the discrepancies and fallacies of the corporate law and the system of fraud check in India.

Let us suppose that:

a) Elder son gets married.

b) Father fells sick and stops attending business.

c) Accounts & compliance is handled by elder son.

d) Elder son possess digital signature certificate of the father in good faith.

e) He also possesses blank signed papers by father, again in good faith.

f) Digital signature certificate and blank signed papers are misused by elder son to make his wife the director. (passed with two third of majority of himself and father).

g) Post this further shares are issued by him to himself and to his wife.

h) All this results in the elder son & his wife being the majority shareholders in the company and also the majority in directorship (i.e. two directors) since the father being ill is not attending the business.

Keeping the above situation in mind, what could you suggest to the younger son to come out of such a situation.

One answer could be that, this is a case of cheating and criminal breach of trust and the matter must be dealt with by the police. The other answer could be that, a complaint should be made to the Registrar of Companies (RoC) to put on hold the said fraudulent transaction and maintain a status quo regarding the said transactions.

All said and done, actually there may not be any fruitful respite to the above efforts. This is due to the two weaknesses, as I pointed out earlier, one being the lack of effective legislation, and the other is the absence of effective implementation of the present law. In case of a complaint with the police, the investigation only initiates after a length of time, and then to prove that whether the digital signature of the father was possessed by the son under deceit is again not easy. It may take years to collect evidence and complete investigation, and in the meantime the business of the company remains disturbed, due to the dispute regarding who shall run the company in the mean time.

And suppose one decides to approach the registrar of companies, the department would actually have to investigate the situation de-novo. Since, the as-on-date status of the company cannot be freezed to status-quo, without going into investigation. Again the usual situation faced by number of people in India at this point is, how to carry forward the business under such disputed circumstances. Ultimately, the business suffers and so do the owners of the company.

The above illustration was a true account of more than few similar cases, which I dealt with. I am not blaming the computerization of the Registrar of Companies ("RoC") office entirely for this, which was done in February 2006. But the truth is that the loopholes still remain in the RoC system itself. In the context of India, the system of digital signature and e-filing, and reliability of the same is totally different as compared to some of the countries in European or North American continents.

The Case of Share Transfers: Allegations of Fraud and Forgery

If the majority group in a private or a family-owned company fabricates necessary documents and shows as if certain shares are transferred illegally or certain transaction did not take place at all. What can be the remedy to the same?

The scope for forgery has become ever more than before, with the introduction of e-filing, as it has become very difficult to prove a company to be guilty of an offence, whereby it did not comply with the stipulation contained in the Act as to the filing of forms with the authorities like RoC. The non-filing of the required forms with the registrar of companies, prior to the introduction of MCA scheme or e-filing mechanism, was never considered so seriously. Whereas the listed public companies are supposed to adhere to the conditions of listing agreement and plethora of SEBI regulations, and as such, it is very rare to see violation of the provisions of the Act or the corporate regulations in listed public companies.

It is true that many private limited companies are even not filling the required forms with the RoC as required by the company law requirements. In such a situation where there are no specific laws on the anomaly of non-filing of the required forms, it becomes immensely difficult to infer that an act has not happened merely because the respective e-form is not filed with the RoC. One section of the corporate world believe that filing of e-forms or the required forms with the authorities like the RoC is a mere procedural exercise and not a violation of substantial law.

The big question arises here that whether non filing of the requisite form can go to the very root of the transaction and render it void due to such non filing with the RoC. My research and database search, and interviews of the registrar of companies' officers did not reveal any precedent action by the RoC office whereby action of the company was set-aside or declared illegal on the sole ground that the respective form or e-form was not filed with the RoC. At the most what happens is that the company is put under the tag of disputed companies and the future transactions in the company are put on hold temporarily. In such a case also, the transactions that are already undertaken are not set aside, and only future transactions are barred from being recognized by the RoC.

As discussed above, still many private limited companies or the closely held public companies, function as proprietorship concerns, where the entire shareholding rests with the family members. Due to the family involvement there tends to be lot of difference of opinion in the private companies or the closely held public companies. The will of one person being contradicted and unaccepted by another person leads to situation of hostility. There initiates a series of many hostile actions and counter-actions between the rival groups or among the shareholders. There are instances where it is alleged that the shares are transferred without the knowledge of other shareholders and at times, shareholders also allege that their signatures are forged and documents are fabricated in order to show that the shares are legally transferred. Usually these actions by the majority or the controlling group in the company result in filing of an application under section 397/398 of the Companies Act, 1956 alleging oppression and mismanagement. The company law board has to decide on the issue of forgery and fabrication of documents, as alleged, and a decision finalizes only when the petition under section 397/398 is finally disposed of.

The problem herein is that the company law board cannot go into trial to determine whether the alleged fraud has actually been done or not. Witnesses cannot be tried and evidence cannot be led in Company Law Board (CLB) proceedings. And in absence of such powers the dispute cannot be resolved. CLB's jurisdiction to look into the issues of forgery and frauds in connection with the transfer of shares can be better understood with the caselaw discussed below.

In *Dr.Mahesh Batra and others. Vs. Gujaraj Beverages (P) Ltd., (2004) 5 Comp LJ 550 (CLB)*, the CLB observed that "having regard to the nature of the allegations made by the parties in this case and the disputed question raised on the facts, such disputed questions cannot be decided by the Company Law Board in the summary jurisdiction under section 111 of the Companies Act, 1956. Such questions, which are involved in the present case, can be decided before the civil court on the basis of the oral and documentary evidence adduced by the parties in support of their respective case. In view of the same it is not necessary to go into the respective allegations or the other arguments raised and noticed in the present proceedings".

In yet another judgment, *Tarsen Kansil Vs. Dev Spinners Limited, (2001) 103 Comp Cas 835,* the company law board observed that "on the facts, that there were serious allegations of forgery, fraud, collusion, manipulation and misrepresentation. The petitioner was claiming that the original share certificates were in his possession and could not have been delivered to the respondent-company along with the transfer deeds whereas the case of the respondents was that the originals were placed before the share transfer committee and had subsequently been removed from the records of the company by the petitioner as they were kept at his residence which was the registered office of the company at the relevant time. Similarly the meeting of the board of directors at which the said resolution was approved was said to have been attended by the petitioner and his signature obtained therein whereas the petitioner's case was that his presence had been fraudulently shown. The petitioner had further alleged that his signature on the resignation letter resigning from the post of director of the respondent-company had also been forged. The petitioner alleged that share transfer deeds which were used for the purpose of showing that the petitioner had transferred the shares in question were not meant for transfer of the said shares but were meant for transfer of shares of some other listed companies and respondent No.3 had fraudulently used the said blank and signed transfer deed for getting the shares transferred and also managed to get the petitioner's signature attested on the said transfer deed by the bank manager and witnessed by B by misrepresentation. With regard to consideration paid for the said shares the petitioner's case was that respondent No.3 fraudulently got an amount of Rs.1,50,000 deposited in the bank account of the petitioner by means of two cheques and being the authorised signatory of the said account withdrew the said amount on the very next day, and therefore, the shares having a face value of Rs.10 per share were alleged to have been sold for Re.1 per share and even the said consideration was not received by the petitioner. Such matters could not be decided by the Company Law Board in summary jurisdiction and if the petitioner was so advised he could approach the civil court".

Another judgement on the same issue supporting the fact that the disputed facts cannot be decided by the Company Law Board is of *Bipin K.Jain and others Vs. Savik Vijay Engineering Private Limited and others (1998) 91 Comp Cases 835*, wherein the CLB observed "that, if the company had entered the petitioners' names on the basis of the transfers effected and later removed their names without sufficient cause, then the contradicting stand taken by the petitioners on the one hand and the respondents on the other, relating to various documents relied on by the petitioners, raised complicated questions of fact. If complicated questions of law or facts arise in a section 111 petition which can not be adjudicated on the basis of documents made available, but could be decided only on trial by evidence, the Company Law Board would relegate the matter to a suit. This was a fit case in which to do so".

Similar judgments rendered by CLB are:

Bharat K.Gajjar and another Vs. Castrol India Limited and others, (2003) 115 Comp Case 396—"proceedings under section 111A of the Act are in the nature of summary proceedings, serious questions of dispute pertaining to title could not and ought not to be tried in summary manner and a suit would only be the proper remedy".

Gopalkrishna Sengupata Vs. Hindustan Construction Company, (2002) 112 Comp Cases 166—"that the Board could not act as an investigating authority to investigate whether the signature of the transferror and the transferee on the transfer deed were forged or fabricated, and the same could not be determined in the summary proceedings before the Company Law Board."

The question which still subsists in these circumstances is that, what should be the course of action in case of a family company dispute? Which forum to choose and which agency should be approached for redressal? Police, CLB or a civil court, the decision can only be taken looking into the entirety of the facts. Since some disputes which are of criminal nature need to be reported to the local police. Purely corporate disputes in which there is no alleging of cheating can be taken up to the CLB, whereas when there is crime of cheating and criminal breach of trust involved then one has to involve the Police agencies and file a criminal complaint.

5

Identity Theft

Seemlessly more prevalent in our society than we actually think, identity theft is a crime which more and more people are being a victim of these days. Especially with the electronic transactions being the latest inevitability, the identity theft has been more prone to happen. And the use of internet, which in itself is global, opens even more avenues to the fraudsters to steal someone's identity. You must have heard any of your friend telling you that his or her Facebook or Orkut account has been duplicated and a fake profile is being made on these networking sites using the pictures of their account. It has become so frequent now that known people who are part of your friend list on your social networking profile, use your photographs and information to create a fake profile of you and start misusing the same. And in most cases one would not bother to report the same to the police, keeping in mind the efficiency of our system and authorities in such matters.

Recent reports[1] show that this time around, the unidentified impo-sters managed to mas-querade as the production house, UTV Motion Pictures and dupe the aspiring actors.

The company (UTV) has learnt that the perpetrators not only created a fake company profile on a popular social networking site, but also organised auditions to cast aspiring actors in a film under the said banner. Reportedly, the scam set-up took quite a sum of money from the actors to land roles in the film.

According to Norton Cybercrime Report 2011, globally 431 million adults experienced cybercrime in 2011 and more than 1 million plus adults became victims every day. As per the report, India is fast emerging as a soft target for organized cyber crime with four in five online adults being victims of identity theft in 2011. Identity theft can have serious financial implications, like someone applying for a credit or debit card of someone else and then misusing it to take loans and make payments. Common warning signs of a fraud include unexpected verification call from a bank or a service provider, warning or notice from a bank, unexplained entries in your credit report, unfamiliar purchases in your card statement and debit of small amounts in bank statements—especially the "paise".

One has to ensure the scanning of credit card statements, keeping your personal details safe and keep a check on your credit report to keep the hackers at bay. The common types of ID theft are:

a) Credit and debit cards can be applied for in the name of another individual.
b) Fraudulent bank loans can be applied for in the name of the victim.
c) Phone connections can be taken to carry out forgery and other frauds.
d) A multiple range of debts can be incurred in the victim's name.
e) E-mail IDs and social networks profiles can be created using false information.
f) The information can be used in various illegal activities in victim's name.
g) Applying and earning a job with the victim's ID.
h) Illegal acts can be performed by applying for new driver's licences or passport.

KYC Strong, but Not Enough

Can you imagine how can anyone could possibly take a loan in your name, especially since know-your-customer (KYC) norms are so stringent? Well, here's a piece of news. According to a recent KPMG survey on anti-money laundering, seven out of 10 firms do not regularly update the KYC details of their customers. While regulations require firms to update the data once in two years for every high- and medium-risk customer and once in five years for low-risk customers, only 52 per cent of the firms took the trouble of identifying the beneficial owner who did transact or on whose behalf a transaction was executed, revealed the survey. The report also highlighted the rise in the number of cases in which fraudulent documents were being used for opening accounts.

Identity theft has bigger repercussions also which may involve financial losses. To understand this, one has to be aware

of what identity theft is and how it is used to commit a crime.

Identity theft is a crime whereby a person impersonates the identity of another person and commits a crime, thereby stealing the identity and thereafter committing the crime. Interestingly, this sort of crime is the invention of the twentieth century, the internet and online information system being the keys to successful conclusion of the crime, although the perpetrator in the literal sense cannot steal the identity and he only pretends to be someone else, to get illegal benefits in monetary or other terms.

The person whose identity is used can suffer various consequences when he or she is held responsible for the perpetrator's misdeeds of which he or she is not even aware. In many countries specific laws make it a crime to use another person's identity for personal gain. Also, the kinds of the identity thefts vary among various countries. Like in Europe or US, stealing someone's social security number to obtain employment or government benefits maybe a common form of identity theft crime, while in India or some similarly placed countries, it may be stealing someone's credit card and using the same to make purchases and withdrawing cash.

Identity theft is used to commit crimes including terrorism, illegal immigration and espionage. There have been cases of identity cloning to attack payment systems, including online credit card processing and medical insurance.

In my attempt to find out how the crime which is predominant in the US actually happens and how it is executed,

I came across so many situations where the impersonation of the identity was used by thieves to commit crimes of modern criminal excellence.

Various Types of Identity Frauds

a) Financial identity theft (using another's identity to obtain goods and services).
b) Criminal identity theft (posing as another when apprehended for a crime).
c) Business/commercial identity theft (using another's business name to obtain credit).
d) Identity cloning (using another's information to assume his or her identity in daily life).
e) Medical identity theft (using another's information to obtain medical care or drugs) (not that usual in India).

Financial Identity Theft

The most recent and growing form of the identity theft, which may be called as the crime of the century, is the financial identity Theft. This is a situation most common where the criminal uses the stolen credit card or password and bank account information of the victim to derive illegal monetary benefit in terms of cash, goods or services. The result is that till the time one actually gets to know that his or her identity has been stolen, the same has been used to withdraw huge amounts from the bank account, or ample shopping have been done to leave the person helpless.

Increasing e-commerce and digitization of the data has led to sharing of important information of the individuals being shared with the companies providing online and tele-services. This includes the account number and the password of the bank account, the credit card number and the CVV number being used for online purchases, online filing of the official documents with the Registrar of Companies, Government of India, using a digital signature certificate.

Criminal Identity Theft

Criminal identity theft is a situation where a criminal identifies himself to the police as another individual. In few cases the criminal obtains a state-issued ID using stolen documents or personal information belonging to another person, or they might simply use a fake ID. When the criminal is caught and is arrested for a crime, he presents the fake ID to authorities, who place charges under the identity theft victim's name and release the criminal. When the criminal fails to appear for his court hearing, a warrant is issued under the assumed name. The victim might get to know of the incident only when the state suspends their driving licence, or through a background check performed for employment or other purposes, or in other cases could be arrested when stopped for a traffic violation.

Once you are a victim of the identity theft, life can be really difficult and could render you in such circumstances where it becomes really difficult to clear your record. The steps required to clear the victim's incorrect criminal record depends on what jurisdiction the crime occurred in and whether the true identity of the criminal is known. The victim might need to locate

the original arresting officers, or be fingerprinted to prove his own identity, and may need to go to a court hearing to be cleared of the charges. In such cases authorities sometimes permanently maintain the victim's name as an alias for the criminal's true identity in their criminal record databases. One problem that victims of criminal identity theft encounter is that various data aggregators still maintain the incorrect criminal records in their databases even after court and police records are corrected. Thus it is possible that a future back-ground check will return the incorrect criminal records, which could cause continuous trauma and inconve-nience.

Business/Commercial Identity Theft

Though usually it is very short-lived, it can cause considerable loss of image and also financial loss to the business or commercial entity. When a criminal pretends himself or his firm to be associated, or being part and parcel of another reputed company, to gain credit in terms of goodwill, credit from the bank, obtaining a loan, etc., the said act is a business/ commercial identity theft. Sometimes the criminals may even pose to be representing the reputed company itself, thereby securing money illegally which actually belonged to the victim company.

Practically though business/commercial identity theft cannot continue for long, since one cannot steal the identity of a reputed commercial concern and stay hidden for much time.

Identity Cloning and Concealment

In such a situation, the criminal, by acquiring personal identifiers, impersonates someone for the purpose of concealment from police or other authorities. Such kind of cloning is usually done by a person who wants to avoid arrest for crimes, by a person who is hiding from creditors or other individuals, or by a person who is working illegally in a foreign country. Unlike credit-based financial crimes, concealment can continue for an indeterminate amount of time without ever being detected. Additionally, the criminal might attempt to obtain fraudulent documents or IDs consistent with the cloned identity to make the impersonation being concealed for a longer period of time and be even more convincing.

Medical Identity Theft

Medical identity theft occurs when someone uses a person's name or other details such as insurance information, without the person's knowledge or consent to obtain medical services or goods, or uses the person's identity information to make false claims for medical services or goods. Medical identity theft frequently results in erroneous entries being put into existing medical records, and can involve the creation of fictitious medical records in the victim's name.

This type of crime is specifically active in the European countries or the USA where the medical identity, on being duplicated, really fetches money for the criminal as compared to

India where the concept of medical identity is far from applicable completely. Though with the advancement of the facilities provided by certain private insurance companies offering the medical insurance now in India, this crime could certainly be one of the biggest threats to the common man of India in the coming times.

Techniques for Identity Theft

In order to successfully impersonate another person and stealing the identity of someone, the criminal requires to get hold of the personal information the other person. These fraudsters use the following ways to get the personal information:

a) Remotely reading information from an RFID chip on a smart card, RFID-enabled credit card, or passport.
b) Stealing mail or rummaging through rubbish containing personal information (dumpster diving).
c) Retrieving information from redundant equipment, like computer servers that have been disposed of carelessly, e.g. at public dump sites, given away without proper sanitizing, etc.
d) Researching about the victim in government registers, internet search engines, or public records search services.
e) Stealing payment or identification cards, either by pickpocketing or surreptitiously by skimming through a compromised card reader.
f) Eavesdropping on public transactions to obtain personal data (shoulder surfing).
g) Stealing personal information from computers and computer databases (Trojan horses, hacking and Zero day attacks).
h) Data breach that results in the public (i.e. posted on the internet) or easily-obtainable (i.e. printed on a mailing

label) display of sensitive information such as a Social Security number or credit card number.

i) Advertising bogus job offers (either full-time or work from home based) to which the victims will reply with their full name, address, curriculum vitae, telephone numbers, and banking details.

j) Infiltration of organizations that store large amounts of personal information.

k) Impersonating a trusted company/institution/organization in an electronic communication to promote revealing of personal information (phishing).

l). Obtaining castings of fingers for falsifying fingerprint identification.

m) Browsing social network (MySpace, Facebook, Bebo etc) sites, online for personal details that have been posted by users.

n) Changing your address thereby diverting billing statements to another location to either get current legitimate account info or to delay discovery of fraudulent accounts.

o) Using false pretenses to trick a business (usually through a customer service representative) into disclosing customer information (pretexting).

p) Use of 'contactless' credit card skimming technology to acquire data recorded on special RFID enabled cards.

q) Stealing checks to acquire banking information, including account numbers and bank routing numbers.

Identity Theft: An International Legal Overview

Countries worldwide have been involved in formulating laws for curbing the identity theft within their own perspectives. An important part of curbing the identity theft is related to the stringency of the data protection laws of a state.

The world's first computer specific statute was enacted in the form of a Data Protection Act,[2] in the German state of Hesse, in 1970. The misuse of records under the Nazi regime had raised concerns among the public about the use of computers to store and process large amounts of personal data. The Data Protection Act sought to heal such memories of misuse of information. A different rationale for the introduction of data protection legislation can be seen in the case of Sweden which introduced the first national statute in 19733. Here, data protection was seen as fitting naturally into a two hundred year old system of freedom of information with the concept of subject access (such a right allows an individual to find out what information is held about him) being identified as one of the most important aspects of the legislation.

In 1995, the European Union adopted its Directive (95/46/EC) of the European Parliament and of the Council of 24 October 1995 on the protection of individuals with regard to the processing of personal data and on the free movement of such data (hereinafter, the Directive), establishing a detailed privacy regulatory structure.[4] The Directive is specific on the requirements for the transfer of data. It sets down the principles regarding the transfer of data to third world countries and states that personal data of EU nationals cannot be sent to countries that do not meet the EU "adequacy" standards with respect to privacy. In order to meet the EU "adequacy" standards, US developed a 'Safe Harbour' framework, according to which the US Department of Commerce would maintain a list of US companies that have self-certified to the safe harbor framework. An EU organization can ensure that it is sending information to a US organization participating in the safe harbor by viewing the public list of safe harbor organizations posted on the official website.

Following these efforts various countries have evolved the laws dealing with the identity theft issues. I have compiled below some of the legal answers by various countries to the questions raised by identity theft.

Australia

Australia has in acted different laws for each of the states dealing with different aspects of identity related crimes. The Criminal Code of Amendment (Theft, Fraud, Bribery or Related Offences) Act, 2000 amended certain provisions of The Criminal Code Act, 1995. This was done at the Commonwealth level. The following amendment was made:

> 135.1 *General Dishonesty*
>
> (3) A person is guilty of an offence if: a) The person does anything intention of dishonesty causing a loss to another person, and b) The other person commonwealth identity penalty, imprisonment for 5 years.

The Commonwealth privacy laws are applicable only to Commonwealth and territory agencies, or certain private sector bodies (having turnover of more than 3 $ 3 million per annum or, they deal with sensitive records).

Similarly various stages have in acted there own privacy laws to prevent misuse of data and information.

France

France has also formulating laws relating to identity theft keeping in view the seriousness of this crime and implications which may arise due to the same.

A person who is convicted of identity theft can be find also up to Euro 75,000 and can be sent to prison for a sentence for up to five years.

United Kingdom

Interestingly, the personal data of an organization which may include name, birthday, address, telephone numbers, anniversary dates etc., are all protected by the Data Protection Act, 1998. In an interesting case 5[1] Henriques J. observed that "Identity Fraud is a particularly pernicious and prevalent form of dishonesty calling form in our judgment, deterrent sentence."

In this case the defendant was acting as the "Front Man" in using the stolen credit cards and other documents to obtain goods of the value of £ 10,000 for other persons who were unlikely to be identified ever. The court concluded that the present sentence was required.

Canada

Following strict law and stringent provisions the Criminal Code of Canada provides under Section 403 that:

"Everyone who fraudulent personates any person, living or dead:

"(a) With intend the gain advantage for himself or another person,

"(b) With intend to obtain any property or an interest on any property,

"(c) With intend to code disadvantage to the person whom he personate or another person, is guilty of an indictable offence and liable to imprisonment for a term not exceeding 10 years and offence punishable on summary conviction."

The Privacy Act in Canada, is a federal legislation covering only the federal government, agencies and crown corporations. Each territory and province has its own privacy laws and privacy commissioners to limit the storage and usage of personal data.

The Personal Information Protection and Electronics Documents Act (2000), also known as PIPEDA, is in force and is applicable to further private sector. The purpose of PIPEDA is to establish rules to govern the collection, use and disclosures of personal information, with the exception of the provinces of Quebec, Ontario, Alberta and British Colombia where the provincial laws have been deemed substaintly similar.

Hong Kong

In Hong Kong the law provides the citizens with the right to request the information held by businesses and government. The personal data (privacy) ordinance established the post of Privacy Commissioner for Personal Data who has the authority to issue an order as to how much personal information one can collect, retain and destroy.

The chapter 210 of the Theft Ordinance Under Section 16A Fraud, under the Hong Kong's Law provides that:

> (1) if any person by any deceit (whether or not the deceit is the sole or main inducement) and with intend to defraud induces another person to commit an act or make an Omission which result either:
>
> (a) In benefit to any person other that the second mention person; or
>
> (b) In prejudice or a substantial risk to prejudice to any person other than the first mention person, the first mention person commits the offence of fraud and is liable on conviction upon indictment to imprisonment for 14 years.

United States of America

Being the country most affected by the crime of Identity Theft, the United States was almost forced to draft the Identity Theft and Assumption Deterrence Act. Crimes like exploitation of consumer credit to commit loan fraud, mortgages fraud, credit card frauds, lines of credit frauds, commodities and services frauds led to the Federal Trade Commission taking steps and presenting the Identity Theft Deterrence Act (2003) (ITADA) before the United States senate

The Identity Theft Deterrence Act (2003) now makes the possession of any "Means of Identification" to "knowingly transfer, possess or used without lawfully authority" a federal crime, alongside unlawful possession of identification documents. However, to prosecute the criminal the crime must include an "Identification Document" that either; (a) is purportedly the issues by the United States, (b) used or intended to defrauds, (c) Is sent through the mail, or (d) used in a manner that affects interstates or foreign commerce.[6]

The punishment for such crime has been made strict and fines are also imposed depending upon the nature of the crime {18 U.S.C. § 1028 (b)}, which can extend up to 5, 15, 20 or 30 years in the federal prison.

The ITADA also empowers the Federal Trade Commission with authority to determine the numbers of incidences and the total loss incurred.

Identity Theft in India

Sadly, since years India was lacking in a specific legislation dealing with the identity theft crime. However with the recent amendments made by the government in the law, the provisions are now available to ensure penal action against the offenders. In India data protection is covered under the Information Technology Act, 2000 (hereinafter, the IT Act).

The IT Act defines 'data': "'data' means a representation of information, knowledge, facts, concepts or instructions which are being prepared or have been prepared in a formalized manner, and is intended to be processed, is being processed or has been processed in a computer system or computer network, and may be in any form (including computer printouts magnetic or optical storage media, punched cards, punched tapes) or stored internally in the memory of the computer."[7] Protection of such data and privacy are covered under specific provisions in the Act.[8]

Legal Provisions to Counter Identity Theft

The protection from identity theft has been granted under the IT Act, 2000 under specific provisions. Both civil and criminal liabilities are imposed for violation of data protection. In order to make the law more stringent and bring India on an international competitive front and to use IT as a tool for socio-economic development, employment generation, and to consolidate India's position as a major player in the IT sector the IT Act has been amended vide the Information Technology Amendment Act, 2008 and more specific laws are put in place to check the identity fraud issues:

1) Section 43 deals with penalties for damage to computer, or illegal access to the computer system, diminishing the value of data, stealing or concealing of computer source code, hacking etc.
2) Section 65 deals with tampering with computer source documents, etc.
3) Section 66 deals with the punishment for offences under section 43 of the Act. The Section provides that "If any person, dishonestly, or fraudulently, does any act referred to in section 43, he shall be punishable with imprisonment for a term which may extend to three years or with fine which may extend to five lakh rupees or with both."
4) Section 66C: Punishment for identity theft. (Inserted Vide ITA 2008) provides:

> Whoever, fraudulently or dishonestly make use of the electronic signature, password or any other unique identification feature of any other person, shall be punished with imprisonment of either description for a term which may extend to three years and shall also be liable to fine which may extend to rupees one lakh.

5) Section 66D: Punishment for cheating by personation by using computer resource (Inserted Vide ITA 2008) provides:

> Whoever, by means of any communication device or computer resource cheats by personation, shall be punished with imprisonment of either description for a term which may extend to three years and shall also be liable to fine which may extend to one lakh rupees.

6) Section 72 deals with penalty for breach of confidentiality and privacy. Call centres can be included in the definition of 'intermediary' and a 'network service provider' and can be penalized under this section.

Conclusion

India, being the most talked about country in the world, is moving towards rapid growth and host of opportunities. The extent of business that could be possible to flow into India, in case the protection of data is secured with the legal implementation system, is enormous. Most of the outsourcing work received by the BPOs in India is lower end worked of the value chain. In case India has to exploit to full potential of the outsourcing opportunity, there is a need to move up the value change like outsourcing work in intellectual property rights, such as clinical research, engineering designs and legal research.

Although the law has been amended, the machinery to implement it is the same. Until the law implementation authorities become fully functional and effective, the laws would not make much of a sense alone. Concerns have also been there on the sufficiency of the IT Act and the amendments made therein, however this debate may continue forever. The basic requirement of effective implementation would remain as it is, since they say "A proliferation of new law creates a proliferation of new loopholes."

Notes and References

1. Reported Amrapali Sharma, *Mumbai Mirror,* Dec. 15, 2011.
2. Federal Data Protection Act (Bundesdatenschutzgesetz, BDSG).
3. Freedom of Speech, The EU Data Protection Directive and the Swedish Personal Data Act.
4. Directive 95/46/EC of the European Parliament and of the Council of 24 October 1995 on the protection of individuals with regard to the processing of personal data and on the free movement of such data.
5. *Our Capital vs. Seward (2005) EWCA CRIM 1941.*
6. 18 U.S.C §1028.
7. Information Technology Act, 2000, Sec. 2(1)(o).
8. The Information Technology Act, 2000, Sec. 43, Sec. 65, Sec. 66, Sec. 72.

6

Terrorist Financing

The acts of terrorism in the world have been on the rise, ever since the 9/11 attacks on the US and UK (tube stations) blasts occurred. They have increased in scale and are becoming more multifaceted from the standpoint of objects targeted and methods of implementation. Terrorism has now the opportunity to use the achievements of science and technology for its criminal pursuits. The serial blasts in India in Delhi, Mumbai, Ahmedabad are a slap on the face of the modern civilized (well armed) society.

We may keep on boasting about global peace and harmony, but still the criminal minds are part and parcel of our society, who live amongst us. This makes it all the more difficult to find them and virtually impossible to track their network.

One serious question which arises in such a situation is, how do these terrorist activities get financed? How do the finances and the money reach the terrorists to enable them commit crimes of highest immorality to mankind? Recent investigations in the Mumbai and New Delhi terror attacks have proved that the money used in the blasts came from across the border.

Terrorist financing is a topic that came into limelight after the terror attacks of 9/11 in USA, which than passed the USA Patriot Act to counter money laundering.

Initially the focus was to impede the charities, unregistered money services (i.e., the so-called underground banking or hawala) which were financing the terrorist activities, but now there has been constant effort to bring all the possible areas of threat under tight controls. Global efforts to update and enforce laws relating to combating the financing of terrorism have been made by countries all over.

The prime sponsors of the terrorist groups around the world, the Saudi Arabian charities, are under much higher control and scrutiny, however, there are still miles to go. Most often the terror financing is channellized through Middle East and South Asia.

Terrorist groups like Al-Qaeda, Abu Nidal organization, Babbar Khalsa, Indian Mujahiddin, Jaish-e-mohammad, Lashkar–e-Toiba have been innovating ways to make money to run their groups, organization and illegal activities. Since it is becoming more difficult for terrorists to raise funds from charities, they are now resorting to money laundering.

They are working with drug traffickers, criminals to launder the proceeds of fraud, prostitution, intellectual property theft, smuggling, into terror funds.

Interestingly, the fight against terrorism should actually be the fight against financing of terrorism. If the money used by the terrorist groups is choked, there can be a significant halt to their ability to conduct mass casualty attacks. Also, tracking their financing trail can prove to be an effective way to locate their operational supporters and disrupt their terror plots before they are launched.

In fact, one of the main agendas of the US government after the 9/11 terror attacks on USA has been to curb the terror financing of Al-Qaeda. Ironically, the 9/11 hijackers used US and foreign financing institutions as a channel to hold, move and retrieve their illegal money.

Global efforts to combat the financing of terrorism have received heightened importance over the past few years. Usually the act of financing of terrorism and terror activities involves financial transactions in various jurisdictions and in various hands to make it virtually impossible to track the same.

Unfortunately there are no statistics on what is the exact number or amount of legal money being misused for financing terrorism. Efforts have been made by John Walker 25 (1995) who was first to attempt a quantification of the money laundering in the world. His model suggests that USD 2.85 trillion are laundered globally, whereas the estimates of the International Monetary Fund provides that the size of money laundering could be anywhere between 2 per cent and 5 per cent of the world's gross domestic product. However there is no actual estimate of the amount the illegitimate money in circulation on in the world.

Mumbai Terror Attacks Financing

Attacks in Mumbai have not been uncommon. Mumbai has suffered a series of barbarian attacks:

On 6 December 2002	A blast in a BEST bus near Ghatkopar station killed two people and injured 28. (The bombing occurred on the tenth anniversary of the demolition of the Babri Mosque in Ayodhya).
27 January 2003	A bicycle bomb exploded near the Vile Parle station in Mumbai, killing one person and injuring 25 (a day before the visit of the Prime Minister of India, Atal Behari Vajpayee to the city).
13 March 2003	A day after the tenth anniversary of the 1993 Bombay bombings, a bomb exploded in a train compartment near Mulund station, killing 10 people and injuring 70.
28 July 2003	A blast in a BEST bus in Ghatkopar killed four people and injured 32
25 August 2003	Two bombs exploded in South Mumbai, one near the Gateway of

	India and the other at Zaveri Bazaar in Kalbadevi. At least 44 people were killed and 150 injured.
11 July 2006	Seven bombs exploded within 11 minutes on the Suburban Railway in Mumbai; 209 people were killed, including 22 foreigners, and over 700 injured. [According to the Mumbai police, the bombings were carried out by Lashkar-e-Toiba and Students Islamic Movement of India (SIMI)].

India still suffers from the aftermath of the dastardly and horrifying terrorist attacks in Mumbai that started on November 26, 2008 and continued for three days, killing 180 people, including six US citizens. It was no secret about from where the attacks originated, after the statement was made by Mohammed Ajmal Kasab, the infamous terrorist apprehended by the Indian police, about his origin and terrorist training in Pakistan.

The entire evidence, phone communications intercepted by Indian agencies, evidence collected by the US, Britain and other crime scene evidences led to only one conclusion, that the attacks were planned and executed by the Lashkar-e-Toiba (LeT), a terror organization with links to Al-Qaeda. LeT is listed by the United States as a terror organization. And further investigations revealed that the finance for the terror attacks was provided from Pakistan, although, some reports claimed that the entire attack was financed by Dawood Ibrahim from Karachi, (who is among the world's top most-wanted terrorists), through his Afghanistan-based drug mafia.

While it was unclear to what extent the ISI was involved in planning or had advance knowledge of such attacks, it was well established that Pakistan had exceeded all the limits, by exporting terrorists to create havoc in India.

> Pakistan still financing Mumbai Attack mastermind.
>
> *—16th June 10, Indian Express*

While detailed investigations revealed that Pakistan financed the Mumbai terror attacks, shocking news came up that the government of Pakistan's Punjab province provided Rs 82.77 million to Jamaat-ud-Dawah (JD) and its allied institutions during 2009-10, according to official documents. Since the JuD chief, Hafeez Muhammad Saeed, has been categorised as the mastermind of the November 2008 Mumbai terror attacks by India, there remains no more truth to be revealed.

Out of the said grant by provincial government, over Rs 79 million was approved in the supplementary budget by the Punjab assembly, and granted to the Markaz-e-Tayyaba, the JuD headquarters in Muridke near Lahore. Another Rs 3 million was given as grants to schools run by the JuD in different districts of Punjab, according to the official reports. Reports were confirmed when the Provincial Law Minister, Rana Sanaullah, under a cloud for his links to banned groups like the Sipah-e-Sahaba, admitted that the money had been given to the JuD. He told a TV news channel that the money was given to these institutions after the JuD was "banned" in the wake of the 2008 Mumbai attacks and the Punjab government appointed an administrator for the organisation.[1]

The question on sanctity of Pakistan's claims was raised by the Home Secretary, G.K. Pillai, when he made a statement that Pakistan's intelligence agency controlled and coordinated the 2008 Mumbai attacks. This was the most direct accusation yet towards Pakistan, by India.[2]

> "It was not just a peripheral role,....They (ISI) were literally controlling and coordinating it from the beginning till the end."
>
> Pillai, *The Indian Express*

Mr Pillai, in an interview given in July 2010, had said that the evidence against the ISI emerged from the interrogation by Indian officials of a Chicago man, David Headley, who pleaded guilty to working with LeT to plan the Mumbai attacks.

In May 2011, the same Pakistani-American David Coleman Headley accepted that the terror outfit Lashkar-e-Toiba(LeT), blamed for the Mumbai carnage, got assistance from Pakistan's intelligence agency ISI and both coordinated with each other. The testimony by Headley, a star prosecution witness, came at the opening of trial of Mumbai attack co-accused and his long-time friend, Tahawwur Hussain Rana, a Canadian of Pakistani origin, in the US at Chicago's Dirksen Federal Building. In its opening arguments in the trial in the US, the prosecution said that ISI had links with Rana and Headley. Rana had not pleaded guilty, in contrast to Headley.

The testimony of Headley revealed the following shocking informations:[3]

a) ISI provided help to Pakistan-based terror group LeT.
b) Headley said he first started training in Pakistan more than a decade ago with the LeT.
c) LeT boss Hafiz Saeed, i.e., the mastermind behind the November 2008 attack that killed 166 persons, motivated him for carrying out a 'jihad'.
d) Saeed told Headley that the satisfaction of one second of 'jihad' is equal to "100 years of worship."
e) The LeT operative said he was in touch with 'Major' Iqbal of ISI.

f) Headley, Rana's old friend from military school in Pakistan, claimed that two years before terrorists struck Mumbai, he began laying the groundwork for the attack, financed by USD 25,000 from 'Major' Iqbal of ISI.

The trial of Rana was being closely watched worldwide for what testimony might reveal about suspected links between the Pakistan-based terror group Lashkar-e-Toiba (LeT)– blamed in the attacks– and the country's powerful intelligence agency ISI, which has been under scrutiny after Osama bin Laden was killed by US dorces on May 2, 2011 outside Islamabad.

Headley, an operative of LeT, a co-accused in the Mumbai trial case, may spill the beans about his links with ISI during the trial, media reports said.

The New York Times had reported that the trial of Rana could reveal ISI's links to terrorists and any evidence of spy agency's "malfeasance" would worsen US-Pakistan relations.

Pakistan has been dismissing Headley's accusations against the ISI, claiming it to be as a little more than a desperate performance, by a man hoping to avoid death penalty.

Rana was indicted by a federal grand jury under 12 counts on February 15 in 2010 for planning the attacks, providing material support to LeT to carry out the attacks and guiding Headley in scouting targets in Mumbai in the process.

Rana was arrested in Chicago over the Mumbai attacks. He claimed that he had provided "material support" to 26/11 terrorists at the behest of the Pakistani government and ISI. While Headley pleaded guilty, Rana did not. The court records show that Headley had testified to a grand jury that he had told Rana about "how I had been asked to perform espionage work for ISI".

> "I explained to him that the immigration office would provide a cover story for why I was in Mumbai,"
>
> Headley (court records)

The most shameful aspect of terror financing from across the border was that three of the suspected conspirators named in the indictment were ISI officers.

Headley began working with an Al-Qaeda-linked group in Pakistan called Harakat-ul-Jihad-Islami on the Danish plot after LeT became distracted with the final planning for the Mumbai attack, a plea agreement said.

Sadly, Rana was finally acquitted by the US court from charges of masterminding the Mumbai terror attacks. This came as a shocker to the Indian hopes, which were praying for justice.

The fact that the terrorists specifically targeted US, British and Israel citizens convincingly establishes the point that terror attacks in Mumbai were part of a much broader "jihad" against US, India, Britain and Israel. The problem of Islamic terrorism is global and requires an urgent global approach and solution.

September 11 Financing and US Efforts[4]

The hijackers deposited money into US accounts, primarily by wire transfers and deposits of cash or travellers cheques brought from overseas. Also, several of them kept funds in foreign accounts, which they accessed in the United States through ATM and credit cards. Funds were also received from facilitators in Germany and the United Arab Emirates, or directly from Khalid Sheikh Mohamed as they transited Pakistan before coming to the United States.

The hijackers/ terrorists in the US spent the money primarily for flight training, travel, and living expenses (housing, food, cars, and auto insurance).

The cost of terror attacks by Al Qaeda was somewhere in the range of USD 400,000–500,000 of which approximately USD 300,000 was passed through the hijackers' bank accounts in the US.

Even though the hijackers or their financial facilitators were not experts in using the international financial system, they created a paper trail linking them to each other and their facilitators. Still, they were easily adept enough to manage themselves into the vast international financial system without doing anything to reveal their criminal identity.

Unfortunately, the money-laundering controls that were in place at that time were mainly focused on drug trafficking and large-scale financial fraud, and did not detect the hijackers' transactions. The controls were never enough and could not detect or disrupt the routine transactions in which the hijackers were engaged to cause the terror attacks.

Interestingly, it was found out in the investigations by the US agencies that the funds used by the Al-Qaeda have not been through the personal wealth of Osama bin Laden. Al-Qaeda's funds were sourced around several millions per year by Islamic charities and the use of well-placed financial facilitators who gathered money from both willing and unwilling donors, primarily in the Gulf region.

In efforts by US towards fighting terrorism, the CIA has devoted considerable resources to the investigation of Al-Qaeda financing, and the effort is led by individuals with extensive expertise in the concealed movement of money. The CIA appears to be developing an institutional and long-term expertise in this area, and other intelligence agencies have made similar improvements. Still, Al-Qaeda financing remains a hard target for intelligence gathering. Understanding Al-Qaeda's money and providing actionable intelligence brings ongoing challenges because of the speed, diversity, and complexity of the means and methods for raising and moving illegal money; the commingling of terrorist money with legitimate funds; the many layers and transfers between donors and the ultimate recipients of the money; the existence of unwitting participants (including donors who give to generalized jihadist struggles rather than specifically to Al-Qaeda); and the US government's reliance on foreign government reporting for intelligence.

Reports of the 9/11 investigations brought out that Saudi Arabia should be a key part of international efforts to fight terrorist financing. The intelligence community identified it as the primary source of money for Al-Qaeda both before and after the September 11 attacks. Fund-raisers and facilitators throughout Saudi Arabia and the Gulf raised money for Al-Qaeda from willing and unwilling donors and divert funds from Islamic charities and mosques. However, there was lack of proof and evidence to prove the above facts.

Terrorist Financing prosecutions are still difficult in many cases. The inability to get records from other countries, the complexity of directly linking cash flows to terrorist operations or groups, and the difficulty of showing what domestic persons knew about illicit foreign acts or actors all combine to thwart investigations and prosecutions.

Al-Qaeda's Gold—Easiest Form of Finance

Interviews of the intelligence officers, law enforcement officials, gold brokers, and sources that have direct knowledge of some of Al-Qaeda's financial movements gave a glimpse into the critical yet mysterious role played by gold in the finances of Al-Qaeda, both before and after the September 11 attacks. Gold has allowed the Taliban and Osama bin Laden largely to preserve their financial resources, despite the military attack that battered their forces in Afghanistan.

Diamonds purchased in Sierra Leone and the Democratic Republic of Congo, tanzanite from Tanzania and other commodities were used by Al-Qaeda to make money and hide assets.

But gold being a universal currency, played a major role in transfers of huge money. "Gold is a huge factor in the moving of terrorist money because you can melt it, smelt it or deposit it on account with no questions asked," said a senior US law enforcement official investigating gold transactions. "Why move it through Dubai? Because there is a wilful blindness there."

Since gold is exempt from international reporting requirements for financial transactions, it is a favoured commodity in laundering money from drug trafficking, organized crime and terrorist activities. In addition, Dubai, one of seven sheikhdoms that make up the United Arab Emirates, has one of the world's largest and least regulated gold markets, making it an ideal place to hide.

Also, Dubai is one of the region's most open banking centres and is the commercial capital of the United Arab Emirates. Sitting at a strategic crossroad of the Gulf, South Asia and Africa, it has long been a financial hub for Islamic militant groups.

Patrick Jost, past senior financial enforcement officer in the Treasury Department's Financial Crimes Enforcement Network, said, "All roads lead to Dubai when it comes to money. Everyone did business there."

In addition to using gold to hide assets, there is evidence that Al-Qaeda smuggled gold into Pakistan and India for profit. Smuggling gold is lucrative because the two countries have a high demand for gold, and legal gold imports are taxed.

Dubai's links to suspected terrorist financing and money laundering have long been a point of contention between the United States and the United Arab Emirates.

Terrorist Financing Models

There are various modus operandis that are being used by the terrorist groups around the world to mis-utilize the finances to

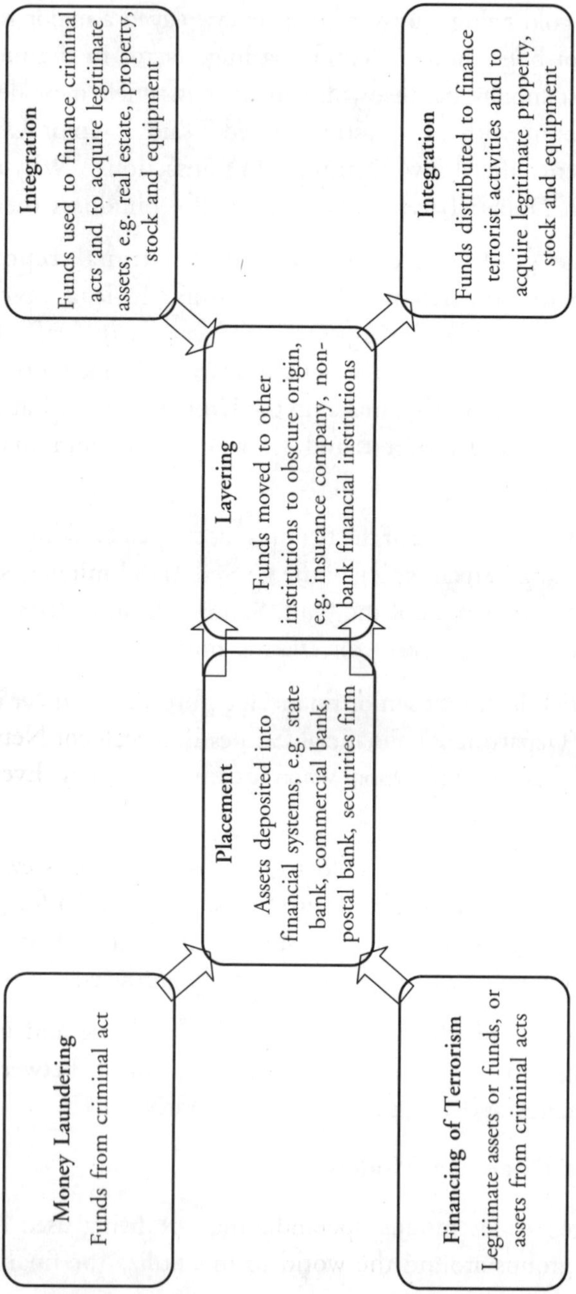

Traditional Terrorism Financing Model

commit acts of terrorism. I have analyzed below, the two common models of acquiring finance to commit terrorist activities.

Traditional Terrorism Financing Model[5]

Placement

If funds have been obtained from criminal activities, this stage is important to get these proceeds into the financial system.

Layering

This stage is all about disguising the audit trail, the source and the ownership of funds. This is important to obscure the links between the sources and the activities that the funds support. This stage may involve transactions such as the buying and selling of stocks, commodities or property.

Integration

At this stage, funds are making their way to the terrorist organization. Funds must be made available so that they can be used to get whatever goods or services are needed to commit terrorist acts.

Alternative Terrorism Financing Model[6]

This model acknowledges the differences between terrorist financing and money laundering, and that funds are but one way, if the most frequently used, to move value. This model is as adaptable as are the terrorists themselves, and accommodates the wide variety of means they use.

Stage 1: Acquisition

In this stage, funds or goods are initially moved into the process that eventually results in their being used by terrorists or direct supporters. Contributors at this stage may or may not know that the final purpose of the funds or goods is for terrorist activity.

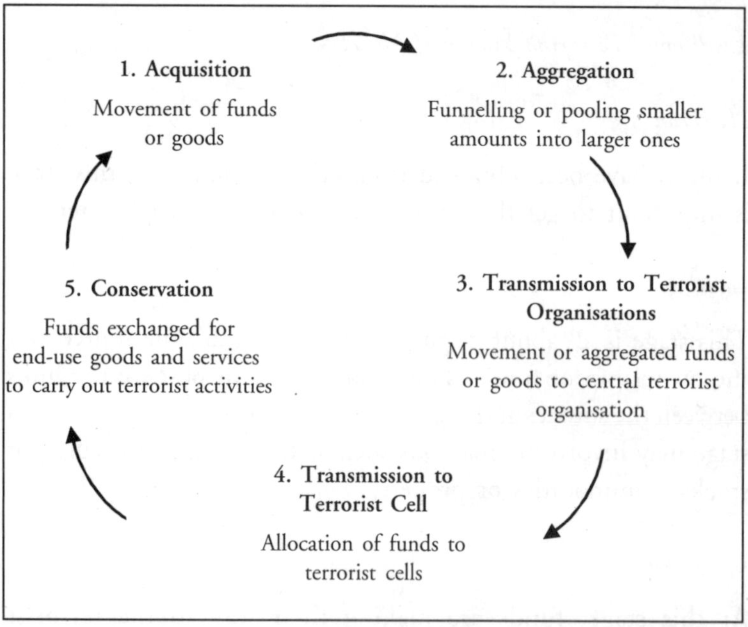

Alternative Terrorism Financing Model

Stage 2: Aggregation

In this stage, smaller amounts of funds or goods are pooled or funnelled into larger ones. This is done by moving them to one or a few financial institution accounts or physical locations. As in the acquisition stage, individuals who combine the funds may or may not know how they will be ultimately used.

Stage 3: Transmission to Terrorist Organization

In this stage, the aggregated funds or goods are moved to either the central terrorist organization or to a designated location, person or group acting on behalf of the organization. Up until this point, some or all of the people handling the funds may not be aware of their intended purpose.

Stage 4: Transmission to Operational Cell

In this stage, funds or goods are distributed to the cells (individuals or groups) that are responsible for carrying out the organization's activities. As with stage 3, the transmissions may occur in one or a number of steps and include the same transmission methods. In addition, methods might include providing cells with debit cards and credit cards if they can readily be used. Logistics play a large part in how sophisticated the transmission method used.

Stage 5: Conversion

In this stage, the funds or exchanged goods are exchanged for end-use goods and services to carry out terrorist activities. End-use goods and services include such things as weapons, travel, training, food, accommodation, fraudulent documents, recruitment, propaganda, bribes and compensation.

Note that not all five stages are necessarily present in every terrorist financing process; nor are they always in the order presented. In particular, conversion can take place at any point following acquisition.

Countering Terrorist Finance

In fact the chain of terrorist finance transaction has many pieces, as that of a jigsaw puzzle. But the problem really lies in the fact that no single agency holds all the pieces of the jigsaw puzzle. The solution actually lies in unified action rather than in individual efforts.

In an interesting finding by PTI, 16 July 2003, the head of Interpol had issued a statement that software and music privacy was being used to finance the terrorist groups. And a joint effort should be made by countries, would over to stop the music and software piracy.

More than 150 countries have pledged to cooperate the fight against funding of terrorism. The Financial Action Task Force (FATF) has led to a cooperative and joint effort towards the fight against money laundering and the financing of terrorism. The FATF is an inter-governmental body comprising the G-7 member states, the European Commission and eight other countries. The FATF endeavors to develop policies that combat international money laundering and the terrorist financing, thereby guiding the banks. Further, it formulates the FATF 40 recommendations which regulate the international framework for cooperative efforts against these financial crimes.

Significant contribution towards formulating the framework of countering terrorist financing is the adoption of eight special recommendations of terrorist financing by the World Bank and The International Monetary Fund (IMF), as the appropriate standards.

The World Bank and the IMF have adopted the collaborative framework with the FATF for conducting comprehensive anti-money laundering assessments of the countries' compliance using a single global methodology. Further, there has been an effort to provide technical assistance to the countries whose financial systems are more at a risk.

Despite all these efforts there has been no respite from the financing of the terrorism the world over. Moreover, there is a need for global cooperation. The FATF also recommends that no financial dealings should be entered into between the countries which do not cooperate in following the standards and recommendations. Other global organizations fighting money laundering include the United Nations, the International Monetary Fund, the World Bank, and smaller groups like the Caribbean FATF and the Asia/Pacific Group on Money Laundering. Countries which keep secrecy about their depositors, like the infamous deposits in the Switzerland, make it further impossible to track the movement of money, once it's transferred overseas. Still, the FATF's uncooperative list came down from 15 countries in 2000 to two countries (Myanmar and Nigeria) in 2005. By most accounts, this is a significant sign of progress.

In an analysis by World Bank of some 50 international terrorist financing cases, the charities and individuals who ran them did not appear on any government-issued terrorist blacklist. As a result, banks had no means to determine whether a transaction that might fund a terrorist attack was suspicious.

One way by which financial institutions might try to prevent terrorist financing is to look at each individual involved in running the charity when dealing with a charity. When opening these accounts, compliance officers should ask for the names of the board of officers and run their names through (know your customer service) that vendors provide. If one of the individuals turns out to be suspicious, then the officer may want to consider not opening the account.

Terrorist Finance—Indian Perspective

As far as the text of this portion of the book is concerned, there is too much to write regarding what can be done to overcome or block terror finances, but sadly there is very less that has been done or achieved. The banking procedures in India are stricter than many other countries, and at many points these are subject to stringent scrutiny. Its true that much of the finance involved in the terror activities may not be routed through the banking channels and may be coming from across the border into India as hard currency. And incidentally hawala transfers in hard cash cannot be easily controlled due to non-availability of documents, since that does not come under banking. According to Indian observers, funds transferred through the hawala market are equal to between 30 and 40 per cent of the formal market. The RBI estimated that remittances to India amounted to $28.2 per cent billion. An international accounting firm has estimated that money laundering flows into India are reported to be in excess of $1 trillion per year.

Still much can be done to create a system under which the empowered government agency formed to combat terror finance raids the suspect individuals, and in the absence of other proofs against them, they at least seize the hard currency recovered from them, because most of the hard currency so received would be unexplained funds. Also the banking transactions of those under suspicion could be kept under a close circuit to find out the dubious and unexplainable transactions.

In the 2008 INCSR report it was stated that India's emerging status as a regional financial centre, its large system of informal cross-border money flows and its widely perceived tax avoidance problems all contribute to the country's vulnerability to money laundering activities.[7] Some common sources of illegal proceeds is the trade in endangered wildlife, trade in illegal gems (diamonds), smuggling, trafficking in persons, corruption and income-tax evasion. India continues to be a drug-transit country.

Use of Drugs to Finance Terrorism

It has now become a known fact that the terrorists use the funds gotten from the sale of drugs, to finance their terror attacks and illegal activities. Recent reports by various journalists capturing the lives of Afghani farmers have revealed heart-breaking truths. The farmers in the areas of Afghanistan, Taliban and a few parts of Pakistan (captured by Taliban) are forced to grow drugs on their fields by the terrorist groups. The farmers being helpless due to their need of earning a livelihood and threat of their life surrender to such terror groups.

The sloggering condition of the economies of these countries is one reason that these farmers are left with no option but to sell "Death" to earn money. The Government of Afghanistan has tried several times to control the cultivation of drugs on its soil, and has destroyed a lot of drug-harvesting farms. But the pre-dominance of the terrorist groups on these areas makes it a daunting task for the government to put a complete halt to the same.

Afghanistan is the world's biggest supplier of illegal opium, which is made from the seed pods of poppies.

Drug-Terror Financing—Indian Perspective[8]

India is one of only a few countries authorized by the international community to produce opium gum licitly for the pharmaceutical industry. Because of India's strategic location between Southeast and Southwest Asia, a significant portion of the heroin seized in India originates in these neighboring countries where opium poppy is illicitly cultivated. Insurgent groups operating in Northeast India finance their activities through smuggling of drugs from Burma into India. Hashish and cannabis intended for the international markets is smuggled into India from Nepal. In addition to diversion from India's own controlled licit opium production, criminal groups produce heroin illicitly for both the domestic addict market and for the international market.

The use of drugs in the Northeast states continues to be a concern resulting in high incidence of HIV/AIDS in the people living in these areas. Seizure investigations suggest that cocaine entering India is being smuggled from West Africa.

The Government of India (GOI) continually tightens licit opium diversion controls, but while law enforcement authorities in India regularly eradicate large areas of illicitly cultivated opium and cannabis plants, a significant portion of licitly cultivated opium still finds its way into the illicit market. India takes many steps to control illegal diversion of licitly grown opium to the illicit market. In past years the US and India conducted joint research projects into means to hold down diversion. India's highly refined methodology to control diversion benefited from this research. India is a party to the 1988 UN Drug Convention.

Although there is no reliable estimate of diversion from India's licit opium industry, some diversion does take place. The GOI estimate is less than 10 per cent of production. There is no evidence that significant quantities of opium or its derivatives diverted from India's fields reaches the US In 2007, the GOI seized 2,226 kilograms of licit opium, which had been diverted, or was cultivated in contravention of Indian law. As of September 30, 2008, GOI had seized 643 kilograms of licit opium out of which 61.62 kilograms was seized by the CBN. As of August 2009, the GOI reported seizures of 2,058 kilograms of opium in 212 cases, 47.28 kilograms of which was licitly cultivated opium seized by CBN.

Action taken by India in 2009 against Drugs

a) India's stringent Narcotic Drugs and Psychotropic Substances Act (NDPSA) of 1985 was amended in October 2001, bringing significant flexibility to the Indian sentencing structure for narcotics offences. After increasing for several years, arrests and prosecutions under the NDPSA declined in 2007. However, the overall conviction rate continues to increase, reaching 50 per cent. In 2006 there were 9,921 convictions, in 2007, 15,390 persons were convicted and as of September 2008, 9,328 convictions were obtained.

b) In April 2003, GOI transferred the Narcotics Control Bureau (NCB) from the Ministry of Finance to the Ministry of Home Affairs. The Ministry of Finance remains the GOI's central coordinating ministry for counternarcotics and continues to cooperate with the NCB. The move has enhanced the NCB's law enforcement capabilities and helped align the bureau with other GOI police agencies under the control of the Home Ministry.

c) Joint investigation by the DEA and NCB have shown the continuing use of the internet and commercial courier services to distribute drugs and pharmaceuticals of all kinds from India to the US and other countries. Although ephedrine seizures within India were down in 2007, one seizure in the US in September 2007 found 523 kilograms of ephedrine shipped through commercial carrier from India through the US and headed to Mexico. The shipment was disguised as green tea extract. In the fall of 2005, Indian Customs seized five international mail packages that were found to contain a kilogram or more of Southwest Asian heroin destined for individuals in the United States, with controlled deliveries leading to the arrest of five individuals in the US. Heroin being smuggled into India from Afghanistan and Pakistan has picked up over the past two years, with West Africans often arrested as the carriers. This trend may continue as the border between Pakistan and India opens up to increasing commerce and travel. Although there have been fewer large seizures over the past year, the number of smaller seizures associated with couriers attempting to travel through India has increased.

d) India is a party to the 1961 UN Single Convention on Narcotic Drugs and its 1972 Protocol, the 1971 UN Convention on Psychotropic Substances, and the 1988 UN Drug Convention. The United States and India are parties to a Mutual Legal Assistance Treaty (MLAT) which entered into force in October 2005. India entered into bilateral agreements with several countries including the United States on cooperation in drug related matters.

Of greater concern was the discovery of more than 6,500 hectares of illicit opium cultivation in two districts of West Bengal (Murshidabad and Nadia). CBN and West Bengal police destroyed the crop in March 2007, but the size of the area of cultivation raises concerns that local farmers have joined hands with larger, more organized drug syndicates, and that an effective law enforcement presence has been absent. All together, the GOI reported that it destroyed 20,001 acres of illicit opium poppy plants in 2006/07, greatly exceeding the amount reported destroyed in previous years.

Although trafficking patterns appear to be changing, India historically has been an important transit area for Southwest Asia heroin from Afghanistan and Pakistan and, to a lesser degree, from Southeast Asia–Burma, Thailand, and Laos. India's heroin seizures from these two regions continue to provide evidence of India's transshipment role. Most heroin transiting India appeared bound for Europe. Seizures of Southwest Asian heroin made in New Delhi and Mumbai tend to reinforce this assessment. However, the bulk of heroin seized in the past two years has been of domestic origin, was seized in South India, and was apparently destined for Sri Lanka. Traffickers who maintain familial and/or tribal ties to Pakistan and Afghanistan are responsible for most of the smuggling of Pakistani or Afghan heroin into India.

India's Effort towards Curbing Terrorist Financing

a) On February 12, 2010 the SEBI issued a Master Circular[9] to all Intermediaries registered with SEBI, under Section 12 of the SEBI Act, on Anti Money Laundering Standards/ Combating Financing of Terrorism /Obligations of Securities Market Intermediaries under the Prevention of Money Laundering Act, 2002 and rules framed thereunder. SEBI has issued over past some time, necessary directives covering issues related to Know Your Client (KYC) norms, Anti- Money Laundering (AML), Client Due Diligence (CDD) and Combating Financing of Terrorism (CFT). These directives lay down the minimum requirements and it is emphasised that the intermediaries may, according to their requirements, specify additional disclosures to be made by clients to address concerns of money laundering and suspicious transactions undertaken by clients. Directives to all intermediaries under Section 12 of the SEBI Act are also issued in the context of compliance with the standards set by the Financial Action Task Force (FATF) on AML and CFT.

b) The RBI[10] has advised that suspicious transaction should include inter alia transactions which give rise to a reasonable ground of suspicion that these may involve financing of the activities relating to terrorism. Banks are advised by the RBI to develop suitable mechanism through appropriate policy framework for enhanced monitoring of accounts suspected of having terrorist links and swift 19 identification of the transactions and making suitable reports to the Financial Intelligence Unit–India (FIU-IND) on priority.

As and when the list of individuals and entities, approved by Security Council Committee established pursuant to various United Nations' Security Council Resolutions (UNSCRs), are received from Government of India, the Reserve Bank circulates these to all banks and financial institutions. Banks/financial institutions have been directed to ensure to update the consolidated list of individuals and entities as circulated by the Reserve Bank.

Banks are advised that before opening any new account it should be ensured that the name(s) of the proposed customer does not appear in the list. Further, banks should scan all existing accounts to ensure that no account is held by or linked to any of the entities or individuals included in the list. Full details of accounts bearing resemblance with any of the individuals/entities in the list should immediately be intimated to RBI and FIU-IND. It is also made a directive to take into account risks arising from the deficiencies in AML/CFT regime of certain jurisdictions viz. Iran, Uzbekistan, Pakistan, Turkmenistan and Sao Tome and Principe, as identified in FATF Statement of February 25, 2009 circulated[11] to banks by RBI.

c) On 1 March 2009 US has cautioned that the hawala money in India is directly linked to terrorist financing and has suggested to New Delhi to strengthen its anti-money laundering and counter terrorism-finance legislations. It also recommended that New Delhi should work towards becoming a full-fledged member of Financial Action Task Force (FATF), an inter–governmental body for development of policies to combat money laundering and terrorist financing.

d) On September 7, 2005[12], India and the European Union decided to work towards blocking access to terrorist financing and cooperate in the fight against money laundering. A two-page political declaration issued after India-EU summit led by Prime Minister Manmohan Singh and his British counterpart Tony Blair said that the two sides will work closely to promote effective multilateralism and strengthen UN peacekeeping and peace building through exchanging best practices and engaging in joint training. They agreed to establish contacts between Indian and EU counter-terrorism coordinators.

e) On 28th February, 2007, India and the US[13] decided to step up their coordination in countering terrorism and targeting sources of terrorist financing—a crucial issue for New Delhi, especially after the disclosure about stock exchanges being manipulated to fund Pakistan-based terrorists. The effort came within two weeks after the bomb explosions in the friendship train between India and Pakistan, i.e., Delhi-Attari express that killed 68 people.

f) The Indo-US joint working group on counter-terrorism, discussed a series of 'cooperative strategies' to fight the global scourge of terrorism. The terrorist finance and money laundering, the ideological dimensions of terrorism, information sharing and widened cooperation for preventing terrorist acts, were also discussed.

g) In January 2008[14], British Prime Minister Gordon Brown on his visit to New Delhi called for greater cooperation with India on combatting terrorism. It wants India to become a member of an international body that counters terrorist financing—the Financial Action Task Force, of which India is not a member yet.

h) On a report by the US treasury to the congress on assets of the terrorist countries and international terrorism program designers in the United States as per the report the amount of blocked funds pertaining to terrorist groups and individuals, totalled over $ 20.7 million in 2007, as compared to $ 16.4 million in 2006. In fact in may 2008 the UN monitoring team reported that $ 85 million A l-Qaeda funds were freezed world over by almost 36 countries.

i) Investigations into the Delhi serial blasts of September 2008 have revealed international links of the alleged militants behind the blasts. The police tried tracking many foreign nationals that were "frequently called" by the alleged mastermind of the Delhi serial blasts. The mobiles that were seized by the police gave vital clues in forming the links to foreign sources of money used in the blasts. The call records of the SIM numbers used by the alleged militants had details of calls made to foreign countries. Officials said 15 calls had been made from the mobiles to Dubai, Vietnam, Saudia Arabia and Malaysia. The police were not able to trace the exact source of funding that goes into arranging basic amenities, living facilities, arranging materials for making bombs and other arrangements for the execution of serial bomb blasts.

j) The Directorate of Enforcement's (ED) officials have been working overtime to trace the funding sources of terrorists and militants organisations through hawala channels. After the replacement of the Foreign Exchange Regulation Act (FERA) with the Foreign Exchange Management Act, (FEMA) all that ED could do was to collate information, since hawala was no longer a criminal offence in India. The ED had therefore, decided to make a representation before the Government of India to once again make hawala a criminal offence or at least introduce a legislation on money-laundering to plug this loophole. However, The Prevention of Money Laundering Act, 2002 which forms the core of the legal framework put in place by India to combat money laundering came into force on 1 July, 2005.

k) Besides the Jain hawala case and the Red Fort shoot out in Delhi, the ED had come across several more cases where terrorists received funds through hawala channels. Investigations into the Red Fort shoot-out revealed an intricate network of front organisations, including a computer institute, through which money was laundered before finding its way into the hands of Kashmiri militants. The case led to several other channels used for funding such activities.

In fact, there is a need to enforce an anti-terrorism drive and condemn terrorist financing at a global level. United efforts and cooperation could be the only possible option left with the civilized society to gage a war against the heinous terrorist minds.

Notes and References

1. *Indian Express,* 16 June 2010.
2. Reuters, 14 July, 2010.
3. *Indian Daily*, 24.05.2011.
4. http://www.9-11commission.gov/staff_statements/911_TerrFin_Monograph.pdf.
5. World Bank, 2004.

6. Adapted from J. Schmidt, ITAC Intelligence Assessment: A Terrorist Financing/Resourcing Model, August 15, 2008.
7. The 2008 International Narcotics Control Strategy Report (INCSR) is an annual report by the Department of State to Congress prepared in accordance with the Foreign Assistance Act of US.
8. United States, Department of State, Bureau for International Narcotics and Law Enforcement Affairs International Narcotics Control Strategy Report, 2010.
9. ISD/AML/CIR-1/2010 issued by SEBI.
10. RBI/ 2009-10/73 (DBOD. AML. BC. No. 2/14 .01.001/2009-10) Master Circular issued by RBI on 1, July 2009.
11. Circular letter DBOD.AML. No.20716/14.01.027/2008-09 dated June 03, 2009 by RBI.
12. Press Trust of India.
13. http://www.nerve.in/news:25350036110.
14. http://in.reuters.com/article/idINIndia-31493220080120.
15. PTI, 25 September, 2008.

7

Hawala—Illegal Money Transfer

"Hawala" means "transfer" in Arabic language; in other contexts the word "hawala" is used synonymously with "trust," usually to express the personal connection between participants and the informal nature of the transactions.

In reality, hawala is a transfer or remittance from one party to another, without use of a formal financial institution such as a bank or money exchange, and is, in this sense, an "informal" transaction. Hawala transactions work internationally, with instances such as worker remittances to their home countries. More often hawala involves more than one currency and entails principals and intermediaries. To accommodate requests of the principals, the intermediaries usually take financial positions. Later, much as in the case of conventional banking practices, these transactions will be cleared amongst the units to balance their books.

Here, I have not tried to pen down the law to check hawala, but rather evaluate the operational modus in working system of hawala. A typical hawala transaction often involves an expatriate remittance. For example, an expatriate Pakistani worker in the United Arab Emirates wishes to send money back home. To do this he goes to an intermediary, the *hawaladar*, to arrange the transfer. He makes payment in dollars or other convertible currency. The hawaladar in the UAE contacts a counterpart in Pakistan, who makes payment in rupees to the remitter's family or other beneficiary. Obviously, some network of family or connections among hawaladars is required to make such a system work on a large-scale and ongoing basis.[1]

It is important to note that although the remitter in this case wished money be sent to a distinct location, no money actually crossed the border physically and no money necessarily entered the conventional or official banking system (unless of course the Pakistani recipient decided to place it there). The transaction rests upon a single communication between hawaladars and is often not recorded or guaranteed by a written contract. The trust between the two hawaladars secures the debt and allows the debt to stand with no legal means of reclamation. There is an implicit guarantee on payments because a broken trust would result in community ostracism constituting economic suicide for the hawaladar (Jost and Sandhu 2002).

Typically, individuals use the hawala system to take advantage of the low cost and quick delivery that the system provides. For the blue-collared worker who transfers a monthly stipend of $100, the unofficial hawala is a far cheaper way to send money back home than the official banking system, at a rate of around 1 per cent of the amount transferred. Because of its low overhead costs, hawala provides a more favorable market exchange rate than the official one. In short, the economic attraction of hawala to the customer is usually the speed, low cost, and reliability of the system compared to the use of established financial institutions such as banks, money exchanges, or Western Union. The system is ideal for use in isolated localities like the tribal areas of Pakistan and Afghanistan where formal financial institutions are rare.

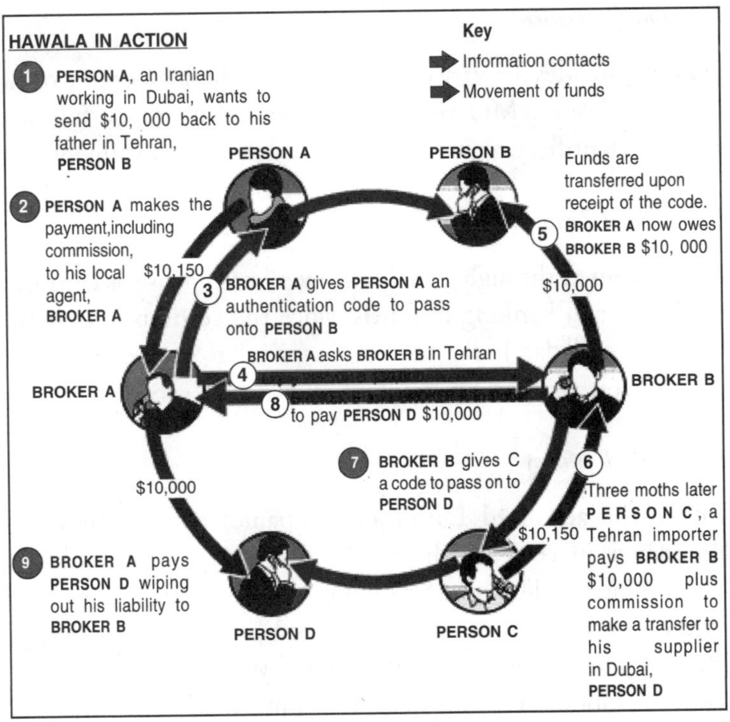

It is believed that the hawala system operates throughout the world, including the United States of America, Europe amongst other countries. Pakistan, India and Gulf countries are considered to be the house of hawala transactions. But Dubai is still handling the largest amount of transactions.

Mostly the hawala transactions do not involve transfer of money or buying and selling of foreign currency between the countries.

Why Hawala?

It is because of the informal nature of the hawala that people prefer its use over the other systems of money transfer. The benefits of the hawala system, although illegal, are many.

Fast and Convenient

Hawala provides delivery of money within the span of one or two days, maximum. Moreover, no formalities are to be followed, such as identification proof or other such legal documentation.

Low Cost of Transfer

Money routed through hawala involves less expense as compared to the normal banking channels, since the commission charged by the hawaladar is far less as compared to the expenses and commission charged by the bank.

Use of Black Money

Unlike the advanced European companies black money is in abundance in countries like India, Pakistan, Dubai and other Gulf countries. The transfer by use of normal banking channels requires the use of the so-called "White Money", i.e., the declared income, whereas in the hawala money system routed through is the black money or the undeclared income. In a country like India where a parallel economy of the undeclared money is co-existing with the national economy, the advantage of using the illegal money is all the more.

Better Exchange Rates

The hawala brokers provide better exchange rates than the official exchange rates since there is no physical movement of the money involved. This is possible since the money is not transferred immediately in physical terms but the settlement between the hawala brokers is done at a later stage by balancing the account.

Lack of Traceability

Being an informal method of money transfer, the hawala comes as a scrutiny-free remittance channels as the inability of the government to regulate such transactions makes the money non-taxable and devoid of other legal concerns.

Reliable Network

The international money transfer routes the transfer through correspondent banks, with the transfer taking a few days. Since the hawala transactions take routes without any physical transfer of money, consequently there is no 'In Transit Money' as the case in official money transfer.

It is due to the benefits aforesaid, that the network of hawala and hawaladars has been growing ever since. Being by far the most private form of transferring money, the entire transactions can occur over a couple of phone calls, emails, text messages. Although the United States requires registration of these kinds of hawala banking services, it is a rare chance to enforce such a requirement because of the difficulty in detecting these transactions. No formal records of the individual hawala transactions are kept usually after the same has occurred. All that exists is usually a running tally of what is owed, often coded and encrypted by the hawaladars. This is far different from the extensive disclosures required by the banks.

Recent Hawala Scams in India

Madhu Koda Scam (2009)

Recently, major hawala incidents in the country include the multi-crore hawala scam involving the ex-Chief Minister, Madhu Koda, along with several other of his former cabinet colleagues. The scam involved Rs. 2,500 crore money laundering which came out as a result of the action taken by the Enforcement Directorate and the Income Tax Department who raided Mr. Koda's house on specific intelligence information. The Enforcement Directorate also filed a case under the Prevention of Money Laundering Act against Koda and his five ex-Ministers. The Central Bureau of Investigation filed an F.I.R. in the disproportionate assets scam. The matter was further probed by the High Court of Jharkhand and special court of CBI under the various sections of Prevention of Corruption Act and Indian Penal Code. Two hawala traders, Manoj Punamiya and Arvind Vyas, were arrested for sending hundreds of crores of rupees on behalf of Koda and his associates to foreign destinations including Dubai, Thailand and others.

Naresh Kumar Jain Case (December 2009)

Naresh Kumar Jain, known as 'King of Hawala', was involved in financing and transporting of contrabands. He was arrested by the Narcotics Control Bureau (NCB) following the inputs from national and foreign agencies, since the drug syndicate run by Jain had national and international ramifications. Jain was prosecuted under various provisions of Prevention of Money Laundering Act by the Enforcement Directorate, alleging that Jain operated a hawala network worth over Rs 5,000 crore.

Jain's arrest was followed by his evading appearance before the Enforcement Directorate since September 2009 when he was booked under the Foreign Exchange Management Act. The NCB alleged that the accused had financed persons involved in drug syndicate in India and abroad. He allegedly laundered money for global terrorist Dawood Ibrahim and also financed the narcotic cells.

The accused was arrested on December 6 and has been booked under Section 24 and 27A of the NDPS Act, dealing with financing drug traffickers in India and outside.

Such incidents are an example of the enormous amount of unaccounted income present in the country, thereby feeding the illegal hawala system.

Sadly, the Government of India has not been able to do much about the hawala money or putting an embargo on the hawala transfers. Although the departments are trying to do their best to curb these transactions, yet the nature of networking, which the hawaladars have, makes it impossible to track the money trail. However, the government has made significant efforts to track down the illegal money, or part of it, which has entered the banking or financial channels of the country.

Moreover, Indian efforts to trace hawala operators involved in money laundering and terror financing are facing hurdles due to non-cooperation of many countries from where the hawala racketeers operate, according to the Financial Action Task Force[2] (FATF).[3]

The tax havens like Cayman Islands, Bermuda, the Bahamas and Switzerland are among the countries which have been unhelpful to India on the issue of hawala. On the other hand, India is now trying to get around the hurdles being created by these countries by strengthening its tax treaties with them.

The global task force in its full report that it prepared after it met top Indian officials from the Finance Ministry and agencies like the Enforcement Directorate (ED), the Income-Tax department and Financial Intelligence Unit, mentioned that this is due to the countries where hawala is not regulated effectively or where hawala is legal. Further, it has been due to the liberalized foreign policy followed by India. The task force came to India in the year 2009 to assess its performance parameters in implementing anti-money laundering, counter-terror financing measures and laws like the FEMA before including India into the top body.

The FATF however praised the Enforcement Directorate's efforts to tackle the cases of hawala. As per the report of the FATF, the ED had inherited some 15,000 cases of criminal activity under the FERA, and had managed to clear about 12,000 cases by end-2009.

All said and done, if the global peace and stable world economy has to sustain, the hawala has to be put to an end. So far as India and other Asian and Middle East countries are concerned much has still to be done and there are still miles to go before they sleep.....

Notes and References

1. Douglas Frantz, *New York Times*, October 3, 2001
2. FATF is an inter-governmental organisation founded in 1989 by the G7 (group of seven industrialised nations) to develop policies to combat money laundering and terrorist financing.
3. PTI, Aug. 29, 2010, 11.25 am IST (*Times of India*).

8

Credit Card Frauds

> "To err is Human, but to really foul things up you need a computer".
>
> —*Paul Ehrlich*

And so is the case that since we are being gifted by the new technological inventions to make life easier, we have also to pay a price in terms of loss of security. Plastic money comes with its own disadvantages, if it has some benefits. In the techno age where a bank employee can now access your private information from his workstation, sitting at a remote location from you, describes the improbable character of the technology.

Recently, I experienced something for the first time that made me realize that the banks are more cautious of the frauds these days, than ever before. My father was travelling to Italy, and I received a call from the HDFC Bank at my residence. The call was to confirm whether the credit card in his name has been used in Italy and whether he is in Italy. I confirmed swiftly, but to my surprise within a few days of his return to India, the bank sent him a new credit card and called us up directing us to destroy the old card. It was on my enquiry that I got to know that using a card in Europe in certain locations has been under surveillance. Since there has been data loss and misuse of credit cards reported, we were issued a new card immediately to avoid any future loss.

Due to such incidents the term "credit card frauds" is more familiar now than it was a few decades back. The Minister of State for Home, Shakeel Ahmad, in his reply to a question[1] in the Lok Sabha said that one of the largest private sector lending institutions, ICICI Bank, lost more than Rs 11 crore due to over 8,000 cases of credit card frauds in the year 2008. There were 8,280 cases reported by the ICICI Bank to the Reserve Bank of India, in which it lost Rs 11.47 crore between April and December 2008. A total of 703 and 2,484 cases were received by American Express Bank and HSBC Bank related to credit card frauds, in which they lost Rs 6.04 crore and Rs 4.90 crore, respectively. According to the data, a total of 12,959 such cases were received during the said period in which various banks lost Rs 36.54 crore.

Interestingly, my research and experience on credit card frauds brought me to the new reality where the theft needs to be redefined.

The definition of theft in the Indian Penal Code Sec. 378 is, "whoever, intending to take dishonestly any moveable property out of the possession of any person without that person's consent, moves that property in order to take such taking, is said to commit theft".

Now with the e-commerce touching its potential market in India, the use of credit cards and ATM cards has gone high from buying airline tickets to shopping through the card. Plastic money is really being used by people more often than before.

And with taking off of the e-commerce in the country, the realm of e-criminals has expanded. And also has arisen a need to bring the modern day crime under the definition of theft. The age-old definition, as mentioned above, sounds too mature and aged to deal with the credit card and ATM card thefts. I came across certain amusing ways, of how these fraudsters undertake their operations.

A Mumbai-Bangalore gang used certain stolen credit card numbers to book online air tickets on leading travel carriers, and subsequently sold them to customers at cheaper rates. This came to light when ICICI Bank noticed an unusual pattern in a credit card user. However, on contacting the card user, he was totally unaware of the ticket purchases. In another interesting case the *Times Of India* reported, two US nationals came to India to set up a call centre in Bangalore which operated in illegal pornography sites. They got credit card details of over 1.5 million users in US and used this to siphon out money through another site. The modus of the crime was that was that Daniel Pena and Bill Smith had websites from which you can download MP3 files. These sites had sub-links to four form sites which were paid sites.

When users of these sites paid to access these illegal sites, the credit card details were misused to access similar sites of their own creation and automatically debit money from them without their knowledge. Pena & Smith asked their Indian company, Customers Connect, to service their tollfree numbers which had been set up to divert their grievances of fraudulent websites in the US. Otherwise, complaints would have been registered with banks in India which would have immediately cancelled their e-commerce facility. Upon receiving complaints and enquiries from the Federal Trade Commission, the FBI and other anti-fraud agencies from the US, the Economics Offences cell of the police initiated action to check the whereabouts of Bill Smith.

Technology to Deception

Though these frauds start often from simple places where one visits frequently like restaurants and petrol pumps. The initial step by the Criminals is to recruit a corrupt bartender, waiter or shop assistant to steal information about a customer's credit & debit card. Usually a pocket-size device with a scanning slot which looks like a pager is used by these miscreants. Such a device can be even worn on a belt. This contraption is called a skimmer. As the customer pays by the card, these unscrupulous employees quietly swipe the card before it actually reaches the pay counter. This copies the information from the magnetic tape on the card to that machine. The customer remains totally unaware of the cloning of their card until they start receiving huge bills of shopping and purchases which they haven't even made.

In an incident reported at Delhi, three persons were arrested by the Delhi police for using fraudulently obtained credit card of multinational companies and using them to make purchases of more than 10 million rupees. The mastermind of the fraud turned out to be a software engineer. They used to forge documents and provide details of different offices, hired for the purpose, to the credit card companies. They used these to buy jewellery at various jewellers' shops all over the country.

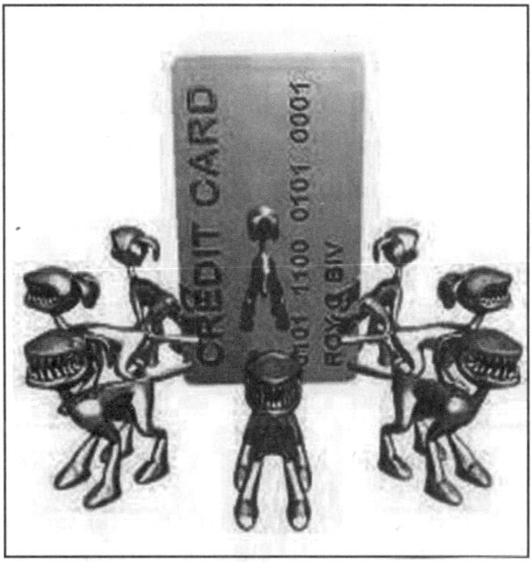

Rather not very surprising that most of these crimes are committed by brains trained in information technology. When a student from a top institute of IT in India was caught in May 2009[2] being accused of credit card fraud and was interrogated about the modus of committing the crime, it came out interestingly about what he actually did. He used to get telephone numbers from the yellow pages, call people posing as a Barclay's Bank employee who wanted to inform them about the free credit card offer. He would then ask the people to give their existing credit card number along with the CVV number to avail the limited period offer. After getting the credit card number, he would call the helpline of the person's credit card company and impersonate as the original customer and ask them to change contact details, so that all queries would be diverted to him. He had good connections with travel agents and would use the credit card numbers obtained to purchase airline tickets online. Cyber crime cell officials said that he used to call people under different names and used false identity cards of Barclay's Bank to get documents from the people.

Preventing the Fraud

Card Verification Value (CVV) or the Card Security Code (CSC)

The Card Verification Value (CVV) or the Card Security Code (CSC) number is a security feature for credit or debit card transactions, giving increased protection against credit card fraud. It is not embossed like the card number, and is always a group of numbers printed on the back signature panel of the card. This provides a level of protection to the card holder, in that a corrupt merchant cannot simply capture the magnetic stripe details of a card, and use them later for "card not present" purchases over the phone, email order or Internet.

"Prevention is better than cure"—this saying is certainly true in the case of credit card dealings. Following tips which I have gathered over my research on the subject could be useful to prevent the loss by fraud.

a) Always ensure that the transaction is completed in front of you and that no details are written down by the merchant.
b) As soon as the transaction is complete, ask for your credit card back from the shopkeeper, to avoid loss of data.
c) Do not provide photocopies of both sides of the credit card to anyone.
d) The CVV which is required for online transactions is printed on the reverse of the card. Anyone can use the card for online purchases if the information is available with them.

Using Cards Online

When using your credit cards for making purchases online:

a) Ensure that the website is a secure site. This can be done by checking whether the site is secured by a reputable net authentication agency like VeriSign.
b) Do not click on links in email seeking details of your account; they could be phishing emails from fraudsters. Most reputed companies will ask you to visit their website directly.

c) Do not give out your credit card details to unknown or suspicious websites.

Stolen Card and Suspicious Transactions

The first and foremost thing to do, after you have confirmed that you have lost your wallet or card or have seen suspicious transactions on your credit card statement, is to call up the bank's 24-hour call centre and deactivate the card or inform the customer service representative about the suspicious transactions. The representative will help you file a complaint in regard to this. In case of lost cards, check if any transactions have been made on the card, and if there are any, inform the bank about the ones that are not yours. This has to be done within a particular number of days which varies between 30 and 60 days according to different banks.

Some General Tips

a) On receipt of a new card ensure that it is in sealed condition and that the seal is not tampered with.

b) Sign on the back of your new card as soon as you receive it.

c) Monitor your account regularly either on the Internet or from call centres. Also subscribe to email and mobile alerts to keep track of card usage.

d) Memorize your card's PIN number.

e) Destroy and dispose of all documents that mention the card number, such as copies of receipts, airline tickets, travel itineraries etc.

f) Personal account information should never be shared with anyone unless payment for the purchase is being done from that account.

Another important thing is keeping any useful information such as card number, expiry date, CVV number, pin number etc. of your cards handy. However, that does not mean that you keep the information in places where it is easily accessible. Protect your card information as you would protect your money.

Finally, always stay at least 50 per cent below your credit limit and review your account information either online or through the credit card company's call centre frequently. This will help you identify any suspicious transactions immediately.

RBI Directives and Initiative

Of late the RBI has called upon banks to enhance customer awareness and to make required investments in suitable technology for security risk mitigation to ensure optimal levels of banking security while delivering appropriate customer convenience. Although the focus is on ensuring a secure online banking experience, the central bank has also expressed concern over the rising number of offline frauds.

The Executive Director, RBI, G. Padmanabhan, while speaking at the Annual Conference on Secure Banking 2011, said that in the IT-enabled banking environment, it has to be recognized that fraud possibilities have assumed international dimensions and that the so-called "safety" must be continuously benchmarked against international standards. The threats which bother the banking sector range from password hacking, card copying/cloning to data and identity theft at various levels of transaction, information storage as well as transmission stage:

a) *Online, Mobile Challenging*: Managing security is more challenging in online and phone banking as compared to other delivery channels. Online threats in the form of phishing attacks, spyware, viruses, Trojans, key loggers are frequent. Threats from ATM take the form of ATM skimming, eavesdropping, spoofing, service denial.

Identity theft in the electronic transactions is a growing cyber crime. Innovative methods of hacking and stealing come to the fore regularly, and the industry needs to take prompt action to safeguard business and customer interest.

b) *Impact of Two Factor Authentication*: The introduction of Second Factor of Authentication for all Card Not Present transactions has ensured greater security in online card transactions, and instances of online frauds has dropped considerably.

c) *Offline Spoofing of Cards*: This has resulted in a significant growth in card transactions in this mode reflecting the enhanced level of customer confidence. However, as a consequence, the focus of fraudsters has shifted to card present (offline) transactions.

He mentioned a case in Hyderabad where fraudsters posing as merchants offered Baskin Robbins/mobile recharge voucher talk time worth Rs.250 against payment of a mere Rs.50, the condition being only debit cards would be accepted. The kiosk machine set up was configured to prompt for PIN and print a charge slip indicating approval of the transaction by the Bank. The Magnetic Stripe Card data and the PIN were captured from the unsuspecting customers and later used to make counterfeit cards for withdrawal of cash. The same modus operandi was used at a petrol pump in Ranchi; only this time, instead of mobile recharge voucher, customers were offered car wash liquid and air freshener. He said that although banks were hardly at fault in these cases, they need to educate customers against such possible frauds.

d) *Alerts*: The Reserve Bank has mandated with effect from July 01, 2011, a system of alerts for all card transactions, irrespective of the channel used. Banks need to ensure that customers are persuaded to register their mobile phone numbers for receiving the alerts.

e) *Phishing*: The RBI also expressed concern over phishing attacks or fraudsters soliciting information by directing unsuspecting customers to a website purported to be that of an authentic institution, through a link in the email. While RBI has cautioned the public through advertisements in the media, banks also need to be watchful.

f) *KYC Process*: The RBI also questioned banks' KYC processes, since in many of these cases money has been paid by the unsuspecting public into bank accounts from where the funds have been withdrawn.

It also emphasized on the need to have effective control over the actions of third party vendors/ service providers, in addition to internal threats as often computer criminals are employees of the same financial organization/bank. So, banks have a new threat, inside violations concerning data at rest, since employees can easily export sensitive files and information via email, FTP or by copying data to portable media. Banks have to control over where their sensitive information is, how it is used, and who obtains it.

g) *Aadhaar Authentication*: A working group was constituted by RBI under the chairmanship of G. Gopalakrishna, ED, RBI on information security, electronic banking, technology risk management and cyber frauds which has has noted that Aadhar biometric data would serve as a secure second factor of authentication even for magnetic stripe cards eliminating the need mandating a switch over to EMV chip and pin card regime, which has cost implications for the industry. The group has recommended that the need for a move to EMV chip cards could be considered after 18 months depending on the progress of Aadhar.

While the RBI is processing the report, it is aiming at a secure second factor of authentication for all card present transactions without being prescriptive about the technology to be deployed for the purpose.

Credit cards, though an easy way to have access to quick money without carrying around a lot of cash, can become a big liability if not used prudently and carefully. One must ensure that the card is used responsibly.

Notes and References

1. February 2009, PTI.
2. PTI Ahmedabad May, 2009.

9

Balance Sheet Bloopers and Hidden Truths in Financial Statements

I may repeat myself, when I say that all that glitters is not gold, but such is the character of our financial facets that I can't resist using the term repeatedly. What I had read while pursuing my chartered accountancy, was a world different from the real balance sheet and financials. And by real I mean "the real" truth behind the glittery or the not so glittery annual financial statements.

The fact is that everyone knows about the trueness of these financial statements. The shareholders, the CAs, the tax officials and not to forget the government all know that what the financial statements reflect is not the true picture of reality, well almost, if not, always. And even though presenting a wrong picture of the financial position of a company is a crime, still repercussions of the same are not one of committing a crime. Sadly though, nothing has been done over the past years to make financial misrepresentations a serious crime in India. Financial misrepresenting is one area which has missed the sight of the law makers for a long time now. After all, this is proved beyond doubt now with the scam of Satyam Computers hitting the IT industry.

I should make myself clear that here, I am not blaming the integrity of the chartered accountants of the country, who prepare the financial statements, rather I am only concerned with their accountability. The body regulating the chartered accountants has been over the years, doing its job brilliantly, but still the same is under constant pressure from the CA community to not to take extreme steps and at the same time safeguard the interests of the chartered accountants. The reason being simple, the governing body of officials is itself chosen by chartered accountants by polling every year.

I have brought out in this chapter, the ways used by the experts to replace the actual numbers with convincing figures, thus painting a fairy picture of the financial statements of a company.

1) Profit Inflation

It's been an age-old practice being followed, specially by the listed companies to exaggerate the profits of the company. Profit is inflated by using different measures, like introducing bogus receipts understating the actual expenses, fictitious sales being shown, etc.

The aim behind the same is manifold. Stock exchange prices are one important stimulant for profit inflation. Better profit means better performance of company, and the same resulting in higher price of shares at the stock market. Listed companies benefit the most known inflation of profits, boasting of high profits means the share prices are bound to rise.

According to the recent trends in the market the prices of the shares have been largely affected by the profit declared by the companies as their financial quarter or six-monthly results. Investors have been investing in the shares depending upon the profit-based performance of the companies, rather than being banking upon the age-old image of the company. The reason is that today's investor is informed and well versed with the market trends. Especially, the internet trading involves the market analysis and reports for various companies, available to the investor just at the click of a mouse.

Well, all this makes higher profits all the more desirable to achieve. This sometimes leads the companies to show fictitious gains or gains which may not be real in their profit statements. A company making decent gains also enjoys the confidence of the market in the financial area. Increased share prices can only be hand in hand with the confidence of the market and the companies.

Another fact which is true, not only for the listed companies but unlisted as well, is not where a company is seeking to get a loan or credit finance sanctioned, it has to show its performance.

And while in financial terms performance is only what your balance sheet and profits and loss a/c shows, the company has to have profits. Due to these reasons the concerns all over the world is the financial history of inflated profits.

Techniques Used by Fraudsters for Inflation of Profit

a) Showing previous year's expenses as this year's income.
b) Inflating sales.
c) Showing loan waiver as income.
d) Revaluing assets to write off losses and expenses.
e) Revaluing assets to write off transfer values.
f) Continuing with dead projects.
g) By sale/lease back of assets.
h) Transferring fixed assets to current assets.
i) Inventory valuation.
j) Change depreciation policies to reduce effect of depreciation.

2) Debt Suppression

A witty comment I read somewhere, "In order to get a loan, you must first prove that you don't need it". Quite true, I must say, that corporates requiring loan can only get them when their financial records show that actually they don't need it. Debt suppression is a tool used by the experts to suppress the debt liability of the company in order to gain benefits therefrom. When debt or loans payable by the company are lower in value, the balance sheet of the company becomes stronger, and along with it the net wealth increases. Let's understand how it works.

Net Wealth= Total Assets - Liabilities Payable

(Say 1000) (Say 800)

Net Wealth = 200/-

In the above example assuming that the debt is suppressed to an extent of Rs. 250/- . Then the net wealth of the company increased as follows.

Net Wealth = Total Assets - Liabilities (suppressed)

1000 - 550 (i.e. 800-250)

= 450/- (i.e. increased by 250)

The benefits derived from this technique are many, some of them listed below:

a) Stronger financial statements
b) Improved net wealth
c) Easier credit finance access (due to strong assets base)
d) Increased share prices in the stock market
e) Market confidence

These benefits, however tempting they may be, are a result of something illegal, and consequently they cannot be called as benefits in the real sense. Miscreants in the financial field have evolved different ways of committing frauds by debt suppression. I have tried to integrate a few of the techniques used by fraudsters to suppress debt in the balance sheet and create a rosy picture of the company financials.

The Modus Operandi

Fictitious Investment

This situation involves the modus where the loan taken by a company is hidden under the guise of fake investments from associate companies, or otherwise, to suppress the debt owed by the company. The loan or debt owed by the company, should be shown under the liabilities side of the balance sheet. However, if the said loan or debt is shown fraudulently as investment by another company into the subject company, the same would not be in the nature of a typical loan liability. And consequently, the balance sheet of the subject company would depict a stronger net wealth. Thus, the suppression of debt in this manner would increase the character of the financial health of the company.

Share Application Money

Another way of fraudulently dressing up the balance sheet is something which has been used by financial frauds in India over a period of time. The loan received by a company, if shown as a consideration towards application for shares of the company, would eliminate the element of debt from the balance sheet. Whereas on one hand, the money actually received as loan is fraudulently disguised in the form of share application money, on the other hand, the money is actually being used for the purposes of the company. When the said loan money is utilized by the company and is no more required, the same is returned to the creditors, while the amount shown in the balance sheet as share application money is eliminated. The same is achieved by showing that application for allotment of shares is being rejected by the company, and the money is returned consequently.

Security to Undertake Future Contracts

Sometimes the debt owed by the company is kept hidden in the balance sheet in the form of security or advance received by the company to undertake future contracts. The financial implications of such kind of manipulation are minuscule. As per the recent amendments in the disclosure requirements of the Institute of Chartered Accountants of India (ICAI), the loan and debt are to be strictly shown as it is. Further, by the amendment in the Income Tax Act, in effect from September 1, 2004, any amount received without consideration shall be considered as income of the assessee. Interestingly, the manoeuvring of loan, being shown as security or advance for a future contract, in the balance sheet will not attract the taxing provisions at all, since, when the loan is actually returned back, the future contract is shown to be cancelled and the amount of advance or security is removed from the balance sheet. The entry passed in the books of accounts is, "Amount of security/advance returned on cancellation of contract".

Transfer of Loan to Associate Companies

In my research, I could lay my hand on the techniques used by companies following doubtful accounting practices, to disguise the true financial position in such a way that even a four-eyed person cannot find out the anomaly merely by looking at the balance sheet. Another interesting way of manoeuvring the accounts and reducing the loans from their balance sheet is by way of transferring the loans to associate companies, sister concerns or bogus firms formed for such purposes. This modus was used by the infamous scamster, Ramalinga Raju of Satyam Computers, to reduce the debt liability of the company, thereby increasing the net wealth of the company. Companies and individuals use such kind of techniques, form various bogus firms and companies, and use them as their vehicle to illegally consume their debt liability into them.

3) Fictitious Expenses to Reduce Company's Tax Liability

This has been the most favourite of all. Financial experts have used this device to hide the income of the companies/individuals over a number of decades now. The profit is deflated to reduce the tax liability of the company and thus less tax burden on the company. Fictitious or inflated figures of expenses are introduced into the financial statements of the company, thereby creating a tax-reducing effect. Consequently the company/individual earns unethical, or rather I should say illegal, savings.

Profit and Loss Account
Money Fraud PVT LTD

Debit	*Effect*	*Credit*	*Effect*
Expenses	↑↑↑↑	Gross receipts	XXXX
Depreciation	↑↑↑↑		
Net taxable profit	↓↓↓↓		

Recently, this technique was used by the scamster of the decade, Mr. Ramalinga Raju of Satyam's Computers, to make merry at the expense of public funds. What he did was very interesting—he introduced a whopping number of 13,000 bogus employees in his company and salaries was paid to them. Those salaries were withdrawn by Mr. Ramalinga Raju himself, being in the name of fictitious employees at the expense of the company. The funds so misused were public funds since Satyam's Computers was, and is, a listed stock exchange company. The company diverted Rs. 20 crores annually on the pretext of fake 13,000 employees. However, the said amount was shown as expenses, being salaries, in the financial statements of Satyam Computers. Thereby an illegal tax benefit on reduction of the profits by the said fake salary withdrawals was accrued to Mr. Ramalinga Raju and consequent loss was born by the exchequer.

The manipulation of reducing the profit to save tax is also done by managing the depreciation policies. Wherein the rates of depreciation are on a lower side, the companies manipulate the depreciation policies to increase the depreciation rates on their assets thereby reducing the profits.

The ways to deceive are endless, but the fact remains that howsoever beneficial they may be, they are all in the nature of illegal gains. The financial reporting practices have grown better over the years, although there is still a lack of stringent penal punishment system in India. And the issue remains that removal of imprisonment provisions and introduction of penalties has done no good to the law and order in India, since the scamsters earn crores of rupees through illegal means and prefer getting away with it by paying a part of it as penalty to the government.

Quite appropriate would be a quote which I read somewhere, "The light at the end of the tunnel is just the light of an oncoming train." At the end of the day, illegal ways of financial accounting have to come to an end. The idea however should be to check the misrepresentation at the time of reporting and to take necessary penal action on the spot, rather than putting the offenders behind bars only after they have managed to swallow innocent public's money.

Cases...

10

2G Spectrum Scam

In 2009, when I conceived the idea of writing this book, I was compelled to study the infamous frauds, though known to everybody and age-old reminiscences from the newspaper headlines which I read (rather oversaw), as a child. But strangely and unexpectedly the Kalmadis, the Rajus, the Kodas, the Citibank Gurgaon Fraud, Hassan Ali's Income tax fiesta, the suspension of IPL boss, Lalit Modi, the Adarsh Housing Ghotala, and the 'external affair' of Shashi Tharoor made my life a lot easier.

LOSS TO THE NATION

₹1760000000000

A Raja deprived govt of this much money in 2G spectrum allocation: CAG report

K S Narayanan | ENS
New Delhi, November 10

THE sheer enormity of the figure, when one learnt about it, was perplexing than enabling to grasp its exactness. The gravity of the offence, though, was evident on Wednesday as Telecom Minister A Raja came under stinging indictment by the Comptroller and Auditor General for arbitrarily undertaking the 2G spectrum allocation, ignoring the advice of ministries, avoiding deliberations of the Telecom Commission — and causing the exchequer a loss of ₹1.76 lakh-crore.

This the first time Raja, the DMK MP from Tamil Nadu's Nilgiris, has come under fire from a top constitutional body during the last two years. The draft report blasted the minister for squandering "a scarce finite national asset at less than its true value on flexible criteria and procedures adopted to

And to add a cherry to my database cake was the scam of 'Spectrum Raja'. The spectrum scam came out to be one of the most popular choices from amongst the nominations of 2010. The year 2010 was one of mass scandals in the history of modern India. We all know that scams and frauds exist, and we live with them all the time. But when they all come out together at one time, they can give any government just a little more tension than a young girl would have on pimples breaking out on her face.

No government before the present United Progressive Alliance has had to deal with a dizzying series of scandals and exposes. Life has been real tough for the man with the most faithful conscience towards his country, i.e. Dr. Manmohan Singh. The man who was confronted with a new controversy every fortnight was defended by his daughter, novelist Daman Singh, in her biography. She said that three attributes set her father apart from the rest and those are clear conscience, integrity and simplicity. But sadly though, India has been suffering from a series of scandals which cannot be controlled by the conscience of one man, howsoever strong it may be.

The latest and the biggest of the scandals relate to the undervaluation of a valuable national resource, i.e. the electromagnetic spectrum or radio frequencies used by mobile phone service providers. The scam roots to the department of telecommunications (DoT) under the Minister for Communications and Information Technology, A. Raja or popularly called 'Spectrum Raja'. The scam was busted with a report of the Comptroller and Auditor General (CAG) of India that was tabled in the parliament on the 16 November. The CAG calculated the notional loss to the national exchequer on undervaluation of spectrum to be more than Rs. 1.7 lakh crore. Now this was big, since the amounts involved were unprecedented in the country. This was the biggest fraud ever. The investigations have revealed that the rules and guidelines were bent in a way which were arbitrary and uninformed to the public.

The recommendations of the Telecom Regulatory Authority of India (TRAI) were applied selectively to benefit a few private firms, sadly there who were without any experience in the telecom sector.

The Story

In 2007, a few sections of the media highlighted how the exchequer was deprived of the huge amounts of auction money due to the faulty manner in which DoT had allocated the licences for spectrum to certain companies. It was time and again brought to the limelight that the DoT and 'Spectrum Raja' had handpicked the directives of TRAI, thereby choosing the most suitable ones. However Raja denied the allegations and claimed that he followed the precedents' as well as the policy guidelines, set up by BJP-led NDA government.

On the directions of the Supreme Court of India, being pointed on the DoT and the report of the CAG bringing out extreme facts about the numbers involved in the scam, an FIR

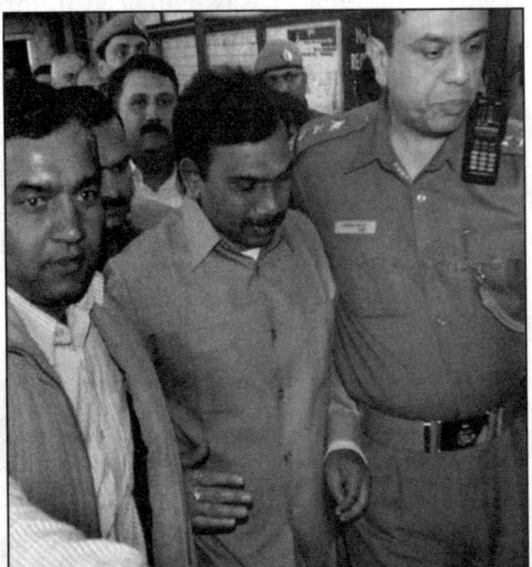

was lodged against unknown persons. The Minister was forced to resign.

The report of CAG could not bring more moving facts than this. The CAG contended that under pricing of second generation (2G) spectrum and the allowance to private companies to use thereby two competing technologies, i.e., the Global System Mobile (GSM) and Code Division Multiple Axis (CDMA) technology under one and the same licence, the losses to the country could be Rs.1,76,645 crore. Further, the allocation of spectrum to companies more than what their licences specified, added insult to injury. These losses accounted for money which was Rs.10,000 for each and every citizen of India or may be over four times the current annual budget of the world's largest social security scheme.

The scams in the telecom sector are not new and they have been there since long, even in the BJP-led NDA government. The books of history containing the dark chapter of telecom scams created by the former telecom minister, Sukhram, in 1996, were finally closed when, in 2009, he was sentenced to three years of rigorous imprisonment for criminal conspiracy. But only a few remember that he barely spent a month in jail before being released on bail. The controversy was initiated during the NDA government when the telecom companies were allowed to shift from licensing regime to a revenue sharing one. Although this was opposed by the then CAG, in July 1999 the group of ministers headed by Jaswant Singh changed the fixed licence fee to a revenue sharing one.

> **"if a hypothetical amount to be calculated, the loss to the exchequer would be about 50,000 crore, at that point of time."**
>
> **A furious Ratan Tata said, in recent statement released to the press***

The Spectrum embarrassment to the government was becoming more evident when the government auctioned 3G licences in 2010. The government gained more than Rs 1,11,500 crore through the public auction of the 3G. However, according to the wisdom of Mr. Raja the losses under the Spectrum 2G were not comparable with the auction prices of 3G. He quoted that it would be as absurd as comparing the basmati rice to rice from the public distribution system. The comments of the CAG stunned the country when it came out that 85 out of the new 122 licences given in 2008 were received by 13 companies which did not satisfy the DoT eligibility criteria. The series of events[1] leading to the factum of the biggest fraud of Indian history are narrated below, and the facts could well stun your minds for the time CBI took to file its first chargesheet in the matter:

Date	*Event*
May 2007	A. Raja takes over as the Telecom Minister.
2007	Process of allotment of 2G Spectrum for telecom along with Universal Access Service (UAS) licences initiated by the Department of Telecommunications (DoT).
Sept. 25, 2007	Telecom ministry issues press note fixing deadline for application as October 1, 2007.
Oct 1, 2007	DoT in receipt of 575 applications for UAS licences by 46 companies.
Nov. 2, 2007	PM writes to Raja directing him to ensure that 2G Spectrum is allocated in a fair and transparent manner and to ensure that the licence fee was properly revised. Raja writes back to PM allegedly rejecting many of his recommendations.
Nov. 22, 2007	Ministry of Finance writes to DoT raising concerns over the procedure adopted. Demand for review rejected.

Jan. 10, 2008	DoT decides to issue licences on first-come-first-served basis preponing the cut-off date to September 25, from October 1, 2007. Later, on the same day, DoT posted an announcement on its website saying, those who apply between 3.30 and 4.30 pm would be issued licences in accordance with the said policy
Oct. 21, 2009	CBI registers a case and files an FIR under various sections of the IPC and Prevention of Corruption Act against "unknown officers of DoT and unknown private persons/companies and others."
Oct. 22, 2009	CBI raids DoT offices.
Nov. 16, 2009	CBI seeks help from the Directorate General of Income Tax regarding information on Niira Radia of Noesis Consultancy and records pertaining to middlemen regarding award of 2G Spectrum licences.
Nov. 20, 2009	Information given by IT department shows involvement of corporate players in influencing policies of DoT via illegal means. Shows Niira Radia directly in touch with Raja.
Nov. 24, 2009	The division bench of the Delhi High Court dismisses centre's appeal against the single judge order which held that change in cut-off date are illegal.
Mar. 31, 2010	CAG report notes that the "whole process of issue of licence lacked fairness and transparency."
Apr. 2, 2010	DIG of CBI, Vineet Agarwal, and DG IT, Milap Jain, who were closely investigating the case, were transferred.

May 6, 2010	Telephonic conversation between Raja and Niira Radia made public by the media
May 2010	Government constitutes GoM for allocation of 3G Spectrum reducing DoT under Raja as a mere implementing body.
May 18, 2010	CPIL and others move Delhi High Court seeking investigation into the case by SIT or CBI.
May 25, 2010	Delhi HC dismisses the petition.
Aug. 2010	CPIL and other challenges high court order in Supreme Court.
Aug. 18, 2010	HC refuses to direct PM to decide on a complaint by Janata Party chief, Swamy, seeking sanction to prosecute Raja for his alleged involvement in the 2G scam.
Sept. 13, 2010	SC asks government, Raja to reply within 10 days to three petitions filed by CPIL and others alleging there was a Rs 70,000 crore scam in the grant of telecom licences in 2008.
2008	Swan Telecom, Unitech and Tata Teleservices sell off a part of their stakes at much higher rates to Etisalat, Telenor and DoCoMo respectively.
May 4, 2009	A detailed complaint is made by NGO Telecom Watchdog to the Central Vigilance Commission (CVC) on the illegalities in the 2G spectrum allocation to Loop Telecom.
May 19, 2009	Another complaint made to the CVC by one Arun Agarwal, highlighting grant of spectrum to Swan telecom at a throwaway price.
2009	CVC directs CBI to investigate the corruption in the allocation of 2G Spectrum.

July 1, 2009	Single judge of Delhi HC holds change of cut-off date as illegal. S-tel had moved the petition.
Sept. 24, 2010	Swamy moves SC seeking direction to PM to sanction prosecution of Raja.
Sept. 27, 2010	Enforcement Directorate informs SC of probe against firms suspected to have violated FEMA. Says can't deny or confirm now Raja's involvement in the scam.
Oct. 8, 2010	SC asks government to respond to the CAG report about the scam.
Oct. 21, 2010	Draft reports of the CAG placed before the Supreme Court.
Oct. 29, 2010	SC pulls up CBI for its tardy progress in the investigations into the scam.
Nov. 10, 2010	CAG submits report on 2G Spectrum to government stating loss of Rs 1.76 lakh crore to the exchequer.
Nov. 11, 2010	DoT files affidavit in SC; says CAG did not have the authority to question the policy decision as per which licences were issued to new players in 2008.
Nov. 14, 2010	Raja resigns as Telecom Minister.
Nov. 15, 2010	Kapil Sibal given additional charge of Telecom Ministry.
Nov. 20, 2010	Affidavit on behalf of PM filed in SC. Rejects charge of inaction on Swamy's complaint.
Nov. 22, 2010	CBI tells SC it will file the charge sheet in the case within three months
Nov 22, 2010	CBI tells SC that the role of corporate lobbyist Niira Radia would be examined by it.

Nov. 24, 2010	SC reserves verdict on Swamy's plea seeking direction to PM for grant of sanction to prosecute Raja.
Nov. 25, 2010	SC ticks off CBI for not questioning Raja. Says it was "beating around the bush".
Nov. 29, 2010	CBI files status report on 2G Spectrum scam probe.
Nov. 30, 2010	SC questions CVC P. J. Thomas's moral right to supervise CBI's probe into the 2G Spectrum scam as he himself was telecom secretary at the relevant point of time.
Dec. 1, 2010	SC directs original tapes containing conversation between corporate lobbyist Niira Radia and others be handed over to it.
Dec. 1,2010	Raja questions CAG findings in SC.
Dec. 2, 2010	Government places recorded tapes in SC.
Dec. 2, 2010	SC comes down heavily on Raja for "bypassing" and "overruling" PM's advice to defer the allocation of 2G spectrum by a few days.
Dec. 8, 2010	SC favours including in the probe period since 2001 when first-come-first-served was the norm for spectrum allocation.
Dec. 8, 2010	SC asks centre to consider setting up a special court to try the 2G spectrum scam case.
Dec. 8, 2010	ED submits report. Says money trail covers 10 countries, including Mauritius.
Dec. 14, 2010	Another PIL in SC seeking cancellation of new telecom licences and 2G spectrum allocated by DoT between 2008 and 2009.

Dec. 15, 2010	Swamy files petition in Delhi Court seeking his inclusion as a public prosecutor in the 2G Spectrum case.
Dec. 15, 2010	Swamy mentions in complaint Raja favoured "ineligible" private companies Swan Telecom Pvt Ltd and Unitech Wireless Ltd in allocating the spectrum.
Jan. 4, 2011	Swamy moves SC seeking cancellation of 2G Spectrum licences.
Jan. 10, 2011	Supreme Court issues notice to the centre on the plea seeking cancellation of 2G licences. Also issues notices to 11 companies which allegedly did not fulfil the roll-out obligations or were ineligible. (11 telecom companies—Etisalat, Uninor, Loop Telecom, Videocon, S-Tel, Allianz Infra, Idea Cellular, Tata Teleservices, Sistema Shyam Teleservices, Dishnet Wireless and Vodafone-Essar.)
Jan. 30, 2011	Government's decision to regularise licences of the companies which failed to meet the deadline for the roll-out obligation challenged in the Supreme Court.
Feb. 2, 2011	Raja, former Telecom Secretary, Siddartha Behura, and Raja's former Personal Secretary, R. K. Chandolia arrested and next day remanded in CBI custody.
Feb. 8, 2011	Raja remanded to two more days of CBI custody. Behura and Chandolia sent to judicial custody.
Feb. 8, 2011	Shahid Usman Balwa, promoter of Swan Telecom, arrested by CBI.

Feb. 10, 2011	SC asks the CBI to bring under its scanner corporate houses which were beneficiaries of the 2G Spectrum. Raja remanded to CBI custody for four more days by a special CBI court, along with Balwa.
Feb. 14, 2011	Raja's CBI custody extended for three more days. Balwa's custody extended for four days.
Feb. 17, 2011	Raja sent to Tihar Jail under judicial custody..
Feb. 18, 2011	Balwa sent to judicial custody.
Feb. 24, 2011	CBI tells Delhi Court that Balwa facilitated transaction to Kalaignar TV.
Feb. 28, 2011	Raja seeks judicial proceedings through video-conferencing stating that he faces threat to life from fellow prisoners.
Mar. 1, 2011	CBI tells SC that 63 persons are under scanner. Raja allowed by CBI court to appear before it via video-conferencing.
Mar. 14, 2011	The Delhi High Court sets up a special court to deal exclusively with 2G cases. Balwa also allowed to appear via video-conferencing.
Mar. 16, 2011	Raja's aide Sadiq Batcha commits suicide.
Mar. 29, 2011	SC permits CBI to file charge sheet on April 2 instead of March 31. Two more persons—Asif Balwa and Rajeev Agarwal—arrested
April 2, 2011	The CBI files its first charge sheet in the 2G Spectrum allocation scam.
April 25,2011	CBI files second charge sheet and court issues summons to Kanimozhi, Sharad Kumar and Karim Morani taking cognizance of the charge sheet.

May 6, 2011	Kanimozhi and Sharad Kumar appear before court and file bail pleas while Morani seeks exemption from appearance on medical ground.
May 6, 2011	SC issues contempt notice to Sahara India Managing Director Subroto Roy, and two others for alleged interference in the ongoing ED investigation into the 2G Spectrum case.
May 7, 2011	Special CBI Court reserves order on Kanimozhi and Sharad Kumar's bail applications.
May, 14 2011	Special CBI Court defers order on their bail pleas for 20 May.
May 20, 2011	Special CBI court rejects bail pleas of Kanimozhi and Sharad Kumar and orders their forthwith arrest saying that there is a possibility of witnesses being influenced considering the magnitude of the crime.
June 8, 2011	Delhi HC rejects bail pleas of Kanimozhi and Sharad Kumar citing that there are certain prima facie evidences against the accused and they may be in a position to influence the 2G probe.
June 20, 2011	SC rejects Kanimozhi's bail plea.
July 25, 2011	Arguments on charges begin. Raja seeks to make Prime Minister and former finance minister P. Chidambaram as witnesses.
Aug. 26, 2011	Special CBI court allows Subramanian Swamy to argue his own case (mainly to address the possible loopholes in CBI investigation of the case).
Aug 30, 2011	The Income Tax Department orders freezing of accounts, attachment of properties worth 223 crore (US$44.49 million) of five companies mainly related to DB Realty under the provisions of Prevention of Money Laundering Act (PMLA).

Sept 1, 2011	ED files status report in Supreme Court, says there have been FEMA violation of Rs. 10,000 crore.
Sept. 15, 2011	Swamy pleads before special CBI court that P. Chidambaram should be made co-accused.
Sept. 22, 2011	CBI defends Chidambaram in SC, blames DoT for all wrongs.
Sept. 26, 2011	CBI moves plea for framing fresh charge for criminal breach of trust against Raja, Chandolia and Behura.
Sept. 29, 2011	CBI says role of Anil Ambani being probed, gives a virtual clean chit to Tata and Videocon groups.
Oct. 9, 2011	CBI files FIR against Maran and his brother in Aircel-Maxis deal.
Oct. 10, 2011	SC reserves order against Subramanian Swamy's plea for a probe into Home Minister Chidambaram's role in the 2G scam. On the same day CBI books former telecom minister and DMK leader, Dayanidhi Maran, and his brother and media baron, Kalanithi Maran.
Oct. 22, 2011	Special CBI court finds prima facie evidence to put on trial all 17 accused including Raja on various counts like criminal conspiracy, breach of trust, cheating and forgery.
Nov. 3, 2011	Special CBI court dismisses bail pleas of all the eight applicants (including Kanimozhi).
Nov. 8, 2011	Special CBI court orders CBI to give a copy of the file on sale of equity by telecom companies (for investigating P. Chidambaram's involvement) to Swamy.

Nov. 9, 2011	Delhi HC refuses to grant interim bail to Karim Morani on health grounds wondering why everybody falls sick once they are is in custody. HC issues notice to the CBI on its reply on the bail pleas of the five accused by 1 December.
Nov. 11, 2011	Trial of the 17 accused begins in Patiala House special CBI court.
Nov. 14, 2011	UPA government moves SC seeking to restrain Dr Subramanian Swamy from making public allegations against the UPA leadership (especially Home Minister P. Chidambaram and UPA Chairperson Sonia Gandhi) in the 2G scam case
Nov. 22, 2011	The Special CBI court shifts the trial to the Tihar Jail complex following a Delhi High Court order.
Nov. 23, 2011	SC grants bail to five corporate executives – Sanjay Chandra of Unitech Wireless, Vinod Goenka of Swan Telecom as well as Reliance Group's Gautam Doshi, Surendra Pipara and Hari Nayar.
Nov. 28, 2011	HC grants bail to DMK MP, Kanimozhi, and four others namely, Karim Morani, Sharad Kumar, Asif Balwa and Rajeev Agarwal. The court upholds the principle of parity under Section 144 of the Constitution of India that upholds an order passed by the SC.
Nov. 29, 2011	The special CBI court grants bail to Shahid Balwa citing principle of parity that SC and HC have already granted bail to 10 other accused.
Dec. 1, 2011	The special CBI court grants bail to A. Raja's ex-private secretary, R.K. Chandolia, and puts additional condition to not visit the DoT without prior permission of the court.

Dec. 2, 2011	Taking a suo motu cognizance, HC stays bail given by trial court to R. K. Chandolia.
Dec. 7, 2011	SC stays HC's suo motu order against Chandolia's bail.
Dec. 8, 2011	The special CBI court accepts Swamy's plea against Chidambaram to become a witness in his own complaint and examine two witnesses, including senior CBI official and senior finance ministry official.
Dec. 12, 2011	CBI files third charge sheet naming Essar Group promoters Ravi Ruia, his son Anshuman Ruia and its director (Strategy and Planning) Vikas Saraf, Loop Telecom promoters Kiran Khaitan (sister of Ravi Ruia) and her husband I.P. Khaitan. It also charge sheets Loop Mobile India Ltd, its subsidiary Loop Telecom Pvt Ltd and Essar Tele Holding.
Dec. 16, 2011	HC rejects bail plea of Siddharth Behura saying "he was the 'perpetrator' of the illegal designs of Raja and would not claim benefit of parity with 10 others released on bail.
Feb. 2, 2012	The Supreme Court of India cancells all 122 licences allotted during A Raja's tenure and imposes Rs 5 crore (US$ 1,018,122) fine on Unitech, Swan & Tata Teleservices. It also imposes a fine of Rs 50 lakh on Loop Telecom Pvt Ltd, S-Tel, Allianz Infratech and Sistema Shyam Tele Services Ltd. It also asks trial court to decide whether Home Minister P. Chidambaram should be made co-accused in 2G scam.
Feb. 4, 2012	The special court of Justice O.P Saini dismisses the plea of Subramanian Swamy to make then Finance Minister P. Chidambaram as a co-accused in the 2G scam.

Feb. 8, 2012	ED registers money laundering case against DMK leader Dayanidhi Maran and his brother Kalanithi Maran for allegedly receiving illegal gratification of about 550 crore in the Aircel-Maxis deal.
Feb. 9, 2012	Essar Group and Loop Telecom approach Supreme Court against its trial before Special CBI Court in 2G case.
Feb. 15, 2012	Supreme Court refuses to grant interim stay on the summonses issued against Essar Group, Loop Telecom and their officials by a special CBI court to appear before it on 22 February for their alleged involvement in a 2G Spectrum scam.
Feb. 22, 2012	CBI lodges a strong protest with CVC on the "dirty tricks" of certain income tax officials to intimidate crucial witnesses in the 2G case allegedly at the behest of DMK's Minister of State (Finance) S.S. Palanimanickam. Dr. Swamy says he will approach Supreme Court on this matter.
Feb. 23, 2012	Subramanian Swamy files petition in Supreme Court challenging the trial court's order which had dismissed Swamy's plea to make Union Home Minister P. Chidambaram as a co-accused in the 2G Scam.
Mar 2, 2012	The government of India files a review petition in Supreme Court seeking partial review of the court's 2 February 2012 order which had quashed 122 licences. The government questions Supreme Court's authority over ruling against the first-come first-served policy but stays away from challenging the cancellation of 122 licences issued during the tenure of A. Raja as Telecom Minister. On the same day former telecom minister A Raja, Sistema,

	majority shareholder in MTS India, Uninor and other telecom companies too file a review petition in Supreme Court.
April 4, 2012	Other than the Government of India's partial review petition Supreme Court dismisses all 10 review petitions. The telecom companies whose review petition are dismissed include Videocon Telecommunications Ltd, S. Tel Ltd, Sistema Shyam Teleservices Ltd, Tata Teleservices Ltd, Unitech Wireless (Tamil Nadu) Pvt Ltd, Etisalat DB Telecom Pvt Ltd and Idea Cellular Ltd.
April 12, 2012	Government files presidential reference in Supreme Court seeking the court's opinion on various issues arising from its 2 February 2012 judgment.

Some losses can be measured in terms of money, while others cannot be done. The loss to the economy of India is far from being valued in terms of money. The loss to the exchequer was valued at Rs.1.76 lakh crore by the CAG, whereas the CBI reported to the Parliaments Public Accounts (PAC) that the loss from 2G could be Rs.50,000 crore.

2G Spectrum allocated to nine existing operators in 2007, despite the number of applications pending for new licences. These included BSNL, Bharti, Vodafone, Idea, MTNL, and the total loss to the exchequer on account of sale of Spectrum at lower prices was Rs.36,993 crore. This was provided beyond the contracted 6.2 MHZ.

The loss calculated by the CAG was based on the offer of Rs.13,752 crore offered by S-Tel in November 2007, to PM and Raja for allotment of 6.2 MHZ of GSM Spectrum for over a period of 10 years. The auction of the 3G licences was taken as a benchmark of how much loss the country could have suffered. The 122 licences issued under 2G could amount to Rs.1,11,512

crore against Rs.9,014 crore that the government actually earned. All further loss of Rs.40,526 crore could have been generated by selling 35 licences under dual use category.

The BJP and left parties had immobilized proceedings in both the houses of parliament for the entire winter session, demanding for a constitution of a parliamentary committee (JPC) probe into alleged irregularities in 2G Spectrum allocation. The Prime Minister, Manmohan Singh, offered to appear before parliament's public accounts committee on the 2G Spectrum issue, in a bid to save the washout of winter session of parliament. However, his offer does not cut much ice with the BJP-led opposition, which pressed for a JPC probe into the scam.

The Parliamentary Affairs Minister, Pawan Kumar Bansal, commenting on how the public money was taken to ransom observed, "Never before in the history of the Indian Parliament has a complete session been washed out without transacting any business. This is violative of all rules of business and ethics, it is rather criminal. Even question hour and private members' business have been made a casualty".

All said and done, the truth is that 80% of the population of this country is not concerned with the scams. And where only 20% of the people of India bear the burden of entire chunk of taxes collected by the government, such non-functioning of the Parliament creates a feeling of dissent and dismay among the citizens.

The question remains: Is law there to be obeyed only by the weak law-abiding common man of India or will the situation ever change?

Note

1. Press Trust of India

11

Satyam Computers: One of India's Biggest Corporate Frauds of ₹ 7,000 Crore

India in the recent years witnessed, what one can think of as the biggest corporate fraud, when Satyam Computers, which is supposedly the fourth largest IT company in India, was exposed of having, for several years, cooking its books by inflating revenues and profits, thus boosting its cash and bank balances; It depicted interest income where no interest actually ever existed. The liability was understated to show greater net wealth and asset base; and the debtors' position was overstated to show that Satyam was too strong a company to be in debts.

Satyam Computers was the fourth largest IT company—after TCS, Infosys and Wipro and ahead of HCL. The promoter-chairman of Hyderabad-headquartered Satyam Computers, Ramalinga Raju, was lying for years to shareholders, employees and the community at large, building up to India's largest-ever 'corporate' fraud of over Rs 7,000 crore.

Interestingly the disclosure of the fraud was made by Ramalinga Raju himself in his so-called resignation letter,[1] where he, in his own words, accepted the crime and the following facts:[2]

a) The company's balance sheet as of September 30, 2008 carried "inflated (non-existent) cash and bank balances of Rs 5,040 crore (as against Rs 5,361 crore) reflected in the books."

b) The balance sheet also carried "an accrued interest of Rs 376 crore which was non-existent, an understated liability of Rs 1,230 crore on account of funds arranged by the Chairman (R.Raju), an overstated debtors position of Rs 490 crore (as against Rs 2,651 crore reflected in the books."

c) Satyam reported a revenue of Rs 2,700 crore for the September quarter of 2008 and an operating margin of Rs 649 crore (24% of revenue) as against the actual revenue of Rs 2,112 crore and an actual operating margin of Rs 61 crore (3% of revenue).

d) This resulted in artificial cash and bank balances going up Rs 588 crore in Q2 of 2008 alone.

e) The gap in the balance sheet had arisen purely on account of inflated profits over a period of last several years (limited only to Satyam standalone, books of subsidiaries of Satyam reflecting true performance).

f) What started as a marginal gap between actual operating profit and the one reflected in the books of accounts continued to grow over the years.

g) It had attained unmanageable proportions as the size of the company operations grew significantly. The differential in the real profits and the one reflected in the books was further accentuated by the fact that the company had to carry additional resources and assets to justify higher level of operations thereby significantly increasing the costs.

h) In an attempt to eliminate gaps in the balance sheet of the company, and as the last effort to save the scandal from being exposed R.Raju had proposed to shell out $1.6 billion from the company to acquire his sons' companies, i.e. Maytas Properties and Maytas Infra. In order to fill the "fictitious assets with real ones" and once the Satyam's problem was solved the payments of Maytas could be delayed. But it created such a furore that Raju was forced to backtrack his move and the deal was aborted.

Implications of the Scandal[3]

On Satyam Computers, its Employees, the Market and the Investors

a) Serious questions were raised about corporate governance, and integrity of the independent directors (Satyam had its share of luminaries such as Indian School of Business dean M. Rammohan Rao, Krishna Palepu of Harvard Business School who resigned and former union government cabinet secretary T.R. Prasad).

b) The credibility of the auditors of Satyam was under serious challenge—the unethical behaviour and malpractices followed by Price waterhouse Coopers (PWC) leading to the regulatory bodies such as Institute of Chartered Accountants of India (ICAI) even considering a ban on PWC's practice in India. Distress signals came from the comparison of the audit fees paid by Satyam to PWC as compared to what was paid by other top three IT majors of India, i.e., Infosys, Wipro and Tata Consultancy.[4] Between 2003 and 2008, audit fee from Satyam to PWC increased threefold. PWC received a consolidated audit fee of Rs 4.3 crore for the financial year 2007-08, around twice as much as what Satyam's peers in the IT industry, on an average, pay their auditors. For the financial year ended March 2008, Infosys paid a total auditor fee of Rs 1.53 crore on a consolidated basis, while the corresponding amount that Wipro paid its auditors was Rs 2.8 crore. Tata Consultancy Services (TCS), the largest Indian IT company, paid only Rs 2.77 crore as auditor remuneration. Thus, for Satyam, the auditors' remuneration on a consolidated basis at Rs 4.3 crore being almost 1.5 times that of Wipro and TCS and three times more than what Infosys paid its auditors was seriously questionable.

c) Satyam being listed on the New York Stock Exchange, and boasting 185 Fortune 500 companies on its client list and NYSE had halted trading in Satyam ADRs (American Depository Receipts), followed by series of class action suits filed by the Investors in Satyam's ADRs in various district and federal courts of United States alleging that Satyam and its top executives violated federal securities laws of USA by issuing false and misleading financial statements.

d) As per the figures claimed by Satyam, it employed 53,000 people. Within hours of the Satyam scandal hitting the headlines, its employees had flooded job portals across the world wide web in search of alternate employment. Allegations were also raised and probe was done to find out whether the company's salary bill of Rs 5,040 crore per year was also genuine in its entirety. Since the number of actual employees on the rolls were considerably less than

what was claimed, it could have been an effective way to siphon out funds from the company in the name of fictitious employees or employees who were terminated long back. Investigations revealed that the fourth largest IT major that always boasted of a head count of 53,000 only had 40,000 people on record in reality. To add insult to injury, the erstwhile promoter and management siphoned off money, at an average of Rs 20 crore a month, payable as salaries, through fictitious accounts, for at least five years before this bubble burst.

e) As for Satyam's shareholders, the stock had gone into freefall before they could even make a decent exit. By the end of the day when the scandal was exposed, large-scale selling by foreign institutional investors, among others, had driven the stock down by almost 78 per cent, wiping out Rs 9,376 crore of investor wealth in the space of a day.

f) Investment banker DSP Merrill Lynch terminated its 10-day-old agreement with Satyam to advise it on strategic options because of "material accounting irregularities".

g) Sebi, the stock exchanges, the Indian Chartered Accountants Institute, the department of company affairs and institutional investors announced a flurry of probes/actions against Raju, Satyam, its directors and its auditors.

h) Raju was arrested on January 9, 2009, two days after he wrote a letter to the company board admitting to fudging the company's books.

i) This was followed by the appointment of a new board of directors for Satyam, i.e., Deepak Parekh (Chairman, HDFC), C. Achuthan (Ex-member SEBI) and Kiran Karnik (Ex-chief, Nasscom).

On August 18, 2010, the High Court of Andhra Pradesh allowed R. Raju's bail application on the ground that all other accused in the same case, including his brother Rama Raju, former Satyam CEO V. Srinivas and three other former IT company employees, G. Ramakrishna, Venkatapathi Raju and Srisailam, were granted bail by the high court.

Against the bail granted by the Andhra High Court, CBI filed a petition to the Supreme Court of India, claiming that Satyam's founder "misused" the bail by meeting one of the witnesses in the case and tried to "influence" him. On October 26, 2010 the bench of Justice Dalveer Bhandari and Justice Deepak Verma allowed the appeal and set aside the order of the high court granting bail to Raju along with his brother Rama Raju and four others, and asked them to surrender by November 10.

The scam-tainted Satyam Computer founder B. Ramalinga Raju has approached the Supreme Court seeking a review of its order cancelling the bail granted to him by the Andhra Pradesh High Court in the multi-crore rupee accounting fraud.

The apex court on November 9, 2010 also rejected the prayer of Raju seeking extension of time to surrender on health grounds and family reasons.

The words of the Hon'ble Supreme Court of India, truly signify the extent and gravity of the crime committed:

> . . . the fraud eroded corporate credibility of the nation.

> Ordinarily this court would be slow in cancelling the bail already granted by the high court, but in extraordinary facts and circumstances of these cases, we are of the considered view that the impugned orders passed by the high court granting bail to the respondents, cannot be sustained in law and the same are accordingly set aside.

The apex court had asked the special court to take up the case on a day-to-day basis and conclude the trial by July 31 next year and asked the Andhra Pradesh High Court not to transfer the judge who is hearing the case in Hyderabad till the conclusion of trial.

All said and done but sadly, no money has yet been recovered and the efforts of the government have only been futile. Even arrest of Mr.Raju and probe into the role of Price WaterHouse Coopers in the scam has not been able to retrieve the lost money to the innocent investors. But, this scam has once again raised serious questionmark into the incapability of the inbuilt fraud protection system of the country, even in the year 2011.

Notes and References

1. Press Trust of India, January 2009.
2. Ramalinga Raju's letter to Board of Directors of Satyam Computers.
3. In.reuters.com, January 2009.
4. *The Economic Times*, January 12, 2009.

12

Chain Roop Bhansali Group of Companies Scam

(which resulted in a loss of over Rs 1,200 crore)

The world of financial crime got a new Devil Avatar, so to say, with this case making the headlines. The frauds committed by the Chain Roop Bhansali (CRB) group of companies befooled almost all. This was a typical case bringing out how easily the CRB group was able to defraud the investors and the regulatory authorities with utmost convenience. This scam took out those pages out of the history books of financial market in India, that told the story of the infamous fallouts of the regulatory system, the role of RBI, SEBI, the Auditors, the Banks specially the SBI, the credit rating agencies, so on and so forth. The master brain behind the scam was an astute 37-year old C.R. Bhansali (after whom the group was named), who stood out for the astonishingly simple methods he employed to hoodwink a large network of institutions and people.

Hundreds of angry, frustrated and scared people stood outside the Reserve Bank of India's Mumbai headquarters under the scorching sun. They were waiting for Chain Roop Bhansali (Bhansali), the head of the CRB Group of companies, to arrive.

Three days prior to this the RBI had given Bhansali 72 hours to come up with a plan to repay his liabilities following over 400 complaints from depositors in his company's financial schemes. The Central Bureau of Investigation (CBI) locked and sealed the offices of the CRB Group and arrested six persons, including four directors (two from Bikaner and two from Mumbai) of the satellite companies of the group, a financial controller in Mumbai and a relative and close associate of Bhansali in Delhi. Most top officials of CRB were untraceable from the second week of May. The CBI also conducted simultaneous searches at 16 places in Mumbai, three in New Delhi, one each in Ahmedabad and Chennai and two places each in Kolkata Jhunjunu, Bikaner and Sujangarh.

Policemen escort C. R. Bhansali, Chairman of the failed CRB Group of financial companies, outside a New Delhi court.
Photograph: Reuters

The Ruined Depositors

Date: May 18, 1997

Post this the CBI froze the bank accounts of the group companies and seized incriminating files and other documents from the residence of the vice-president of the CRB group in Mumbai. By then the rumours had started to spread that Bhansali had fled India and was hiding in Canada or Hong Kong. To catch hold of him the CBI sought Interpol's assistance as well.

In furtherance to the efforts to get to the root of the scam, RBI filed a winding-up petition claiming that the continuance of the CRB Group was not in public interest and the interests of the depositors. The court prohibited CRB from selling, transferring, alienating, mortgaging or dealing in any manner whatsoever with its assets. The group was also restrained from accepting public deposits.

Under such circumstances Bhansali sent a letter to the RBI in response to the legal actions being taken against him. Although, it was not signed by him, the letter mentioned that the RBI order had led to the deterioration of the company's financial position. It added that the company was facing tremendous problems with payments to fixed depositors. The letter further said that "we have, also expressed that in view of the precarious situation which is fast going out of our control, before it becomes unmanageable, our case should be considered sympathetically." This letter to some extent led the investors to believe that Bhansali would come out of the groove and work out a way to get out of the mess. However, Bhansali never showed up.

Background of Bhansali

Born in a jute trader's house in Kolkata, Bhansali was one with studious inclinations. After obtaining a degree in commerce, he completed chartered accountancy in 1980. In the same year, he started a financial consultancy firm, CRB Consultancy.

Through Bhansali's personal contacts, CRB Consultancy soon managed to secure the business of providing issue management services to a few well-known companies in Kolkata. Over the years, he acquired other degrees as well including ACS, Ph.D., MIIA (US) and a diploma in journalism. He then moved to New Delhi to join one of the country's leading registrars of companies. Though he made a lot of money, yet he found it difficult to find recognition in Kolkata. However when Bhansali was caught short-charging the registrar's clients, he had to leave.

Bhansali then established CRB Consultants, a private limited company in New Delhi in 1985. In 1992, the name of the company was changed to CRB Capital Markets (CRB Caps) and it was converted into a public limited company. The company offered various services including merchant banking, leasing and hire purchase, bill discounting and corporate funds management, fixed deposit and resources mobilization, mutual funds and asset management, international finance and forex operations. CRB Caps was also very active in stock-broking having a card both on the BSE and the NSE. The company raised over Rs 176 crore from the public by January 1995. The A+ rating given by CARE and upfront cash incentives of 7-10 per cent attracted investors in hordes to Bhansali's schemes.

The Modus

Bhansali was a master in setting up of dummy investment companies, that had become his specialization. He then used to sell these dummy companies to buyers to make illegal money, defrauding others. He capitalized on the 1985 boom in leasing companies to become cash rich.

With excellent contacts in the Registrar of Companies and the Controller of Capital Issues offices, he registered companies with practically no equity capital and then managed the dummy company's maiden public issue with only a few hundred investors, largely from Kolkata closely knit Marwari Jain community.

After having had a company listed on the stock exchange successfully, Bhansali then sold it for a profit to businessmen who needed dummy public limited companies in a hurry.

a) CRB Capital Markets: Bhansali's flagship company 'CRB Capital markets' was converted into a public limited company, whose main activity was managing public issues. This company went public in 1992 and went back to public another six times by January 1995, raising a total of Rs. 176 crore in three years, compared to Kotak Mahindra Finance, a leading finance company, who over the same period raised less than Rs. 80 crore.

b) CRB Mutual Funds: In August 1994, CRB Capital Markets launched its mutual fund company, CRB Mutual Funds which, through its Arihant Mangal Growth Scheme, raised Rs 230 crore from the market. Another Rs.180 crore was raised from investors through fixed deposits.

c) CRB Corporation LTD: CRB Corporation Ltd. was originally set as a granite manufacturing company by Bhansali, but much of its activities were in finance area. This company raised Rs.84 crore through three public issues between May 1993 and December 1995.

d) CRB Share Custodial Services: CRB Share Custodial Services, another of Bhansali's company, raised a further Rs.100 crore in January 1995 to set up operations.

In the space of five years between 1992 and 1995, Bhansali managed to raise a total of close to Rs. 900 crore from the capital markets (when the market was going through the post-Harshad Mehta scam phase), and he became the chairman of the top three finance companies in India.

Bhansali used his own money to rig share prices in order to raise more money from the markets in two ways: Firstly, he bought his own stock through private finance companies owned by him. Secondly, he used his other public companies to buy into each other as cross-holdings.

For instance both CRB Mutual Fund and CRB Custodian Services featured in the top 10 companies in which CRB Mutual Fund invested in 1994-95. CRB Custodian invested Rs. 15 crore into CRB Capital Markets, which in turn invested Rs.17 crore in CRB Mutual Fund. The latter held 24 lakh shares of CRB Corporation, which again had a 16 crore investment in CRB capital markets.

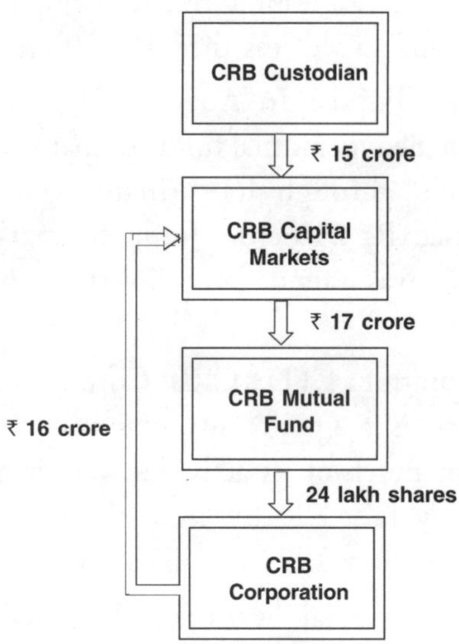

CRB's Investment Coccus

CRB capital markets had invested in the equity of almost 130 quoted companies and nearly a dozen unquoted companies. Bhansali invested in three classes of companies:

a) His own privately owned companies.
b) Private companies owned by his friends and those on the boards of his companies.
c) Many small companies whose issues were managed by CRB capital, but which could not get fully subscribed for.

Almost all of the companies that were featured in the investment portfolio were the ones that Bhansali invested in to generate paper profits for the group. His aim was to buy into IPOs of those companies that CRB Capital Markets could not get full subscription for. Post that he would purchase them back at a much lower price than the issue price and then do a ready forward deal with the finance company, therefore selling the holding at a higher price. Thus he would show profits in the books of CRB Capital Markets or CRB Corporation for the said transaction from the sale of investment. This was repeated by him on a continuous basis creating a fraudulent vicious circle. The illegal benefits accrued to him included an increased price of the IPOs on the stock market and sale of the stock at a profit. Simultaneously, he was reaping the benefit of the paper profits that were accruing to CRB Capital Markets. Higher profits meant that the share prices continued to remain high, which would mean that raising money from the public in the future would be that much easier.

A strong and growing profit-oriented company will get better loans from the banks in any case.

The auditors of the group companies i.e. D.P. Bhaiya & Co and Jain & Swakia were reported to be fake and fraud identities. D.P. Bhaiya's address was actually a collection of open sheds near the Manicktalla crossing specializing in scrap and low quality steel items. Whereas, allegedly Jain & Swakia were a fictitious chartered accountants' firm popular for making any set of accounts to be proper and certified. None of these firms had an address or telephone in their names.

The SBI Duped

a) In May 1996, CRB Caps opened a current account in SBI's main Mumbai branch. The account was opened for intent of payment of interest, dividend and redemption cheques. The payment warrants could be presented at any of the 4,000 SBI branches for payment.

b) However, Bhansali was granted only a current account facility and did not enjoy any overdraft facility. He was expected to deposit cash upfront into the current account, along with a list of payments that had to be honored.

c) Claiming that the logistics of payment were very complex and that it was not possible for every branch to check with the head office before honoring a dividend warrant, the branches gradually began treating these instruments just like a demand draft. These instruments were then sent to the Mumbai service branch, which cleared them and debited it to the company account. The time taken between the encashing of the warrants of outstation branches and then reaching the main branch for tallying was almost 14 days. Once the amount reached the main branch, it credited the branches, which had paid warrant holders out of pocket. CRB took advantage of those 14 days.

d) And for about nine months, the set-up worked really well. However, in March 1997, SBI realized that the account had been overdrawn to the extent of a few crores. SBI alleged that Bhansali had printed 1,800 fake dividend warrants, which were drawn in favour of friends and relatives, and presented at various SBI branches. Rupees 59 crore were siphoned off and credited to these accounts which were allegedly benami accounts owned by Bhansali himself.

e) In the 101-year history of the bank, the SBI had never ever been defrauded on these accounts the way Bhansali had done. Though SBI claims to have informed RBI immediately on detecting the frauds, it took more than three weeks to notify the CBI, which in turn took no action.

The Collapse

The collapse of the CRB group seemed to be a fraud allowed by supervisors despite the regulations in place. The lack of clear communication channels between the banks, RBI and the government seemed to have worked to Bhansali's advantage to a great extent. Frequent clashes occurred between RBI and SEBI in the media, with both of them trying to prove how the other was responsible for not acting early enough. The RBI claimed that it had no powers to examine the asset quality of the CRB group and thereby was not in a position to pass any judgment on the character of asset generation or deployment of the funds raised by the group.

The bank further claimed that the powers were granted only in March 1997, when the RBI Act of 1934 was amended to include specific provisions for the purpose. The bank also stated that it had begun to examine the liabilities and not the assets.

The CRB group came under scrutiny for the first time in September 1996, when it approached the RBI for registration of the group under the NBFC.

Around the same time the Tourism Finance Corporation of India lodged a complaint that the latter was defaulting on its loan repayments. Simultaneously, RBI received complaints from many sources regarding the company's dealings. The RBI, not satisfied with some responses given, launched a detailed inspection of CRB offices through November and December. By February, it had enough information of irregularities in the balance sheets and operations to give a one-month show-cause notice. On failure of the group to give a suitable reply, the RBI placed the ban on acceptance of deposits from the public with effect from 8 April 1997 and also withdrew an earlier clearance given to set up a private sector bank.

Thereafter the post-dated interest cheques issued by CRB Capital Markets Ltd to depositors started bouncing, thereby creating panic among the depositors immediately following the ban. RBI asked CRB to explain how it plans to return the deposits worth Rs.1.39 crore as on March 31, 1996.

The company's interest burden in mid-May 1997 was Rs.8 to Rs. 9 crore per week. Depositors approached various consumer organisations.

a) The RBI filed a petition in the New Delhi High Court seeking the winding up of CRB Capital Markets Ltd when the company failed to respond to the RBI show cause notice within stipulated time, i.e., May 20, 1997.

b) The Delhi High Court had asked the official liquidator to take over the assets of CRB Capital Markets Ltd taking police assistance if necessary.

c) The State Bank of India lodged a complaint with Central Bureau of Investigation for recovering Rs.600 million against which it had the company's Jaipur holding worth Rs. 3 to Rs. 12 crore only as collateral.

d) The Bank of Baroda moved the Bombay High Court for appointment of a receiver to collect its dues worth Rs.40 million.

e) Meanwhile, the SEBI issued orders to the custodian of the CRB Mutual Fund to stop transactions in CRB shares held in custody. SEBI acted after CRB officials did not turn up at the meeting called regarding the next course of action with regard to the company.

Steps were taken to halt the group's activities and asked CRB Mutual Fund not to launch more schemes. The ban was imposed for the second time on the company. Later CRB Share Custodial Services Ltd informed the BSE that it had discontinued services as the registrar and share transfer agent for CRB Capital Markets and CRB Corporation Ltd.

Confusion prevailed since there was lack of clarity on the legal aspects considering the NBFC status of the CRB. Loopholes in the law ensured that the SEBI, the RBI and the Department of Company Affairs had a limited role to play in NBFC's.

It was only in 1995 that the RBI began monitoring activities of NBFCs. After the CRB crash, the RBI was planning to establish norms covering NBFCs better with the market regulator favouring a system through which mutual funds can be monitored better. SEBI was also considering more open disclosure norms for mutual funds and fixed deposits.

The Aftermath

The CRB Scam took the whole nation by storm. At one point, the Union Finance Ministry held a meeting every day to get to the brasstacks of the CRB fiasco. In a meeting with SEBI, the Finance Minister criticized the regulator severely. The government asked the RBI to prepare a panel of auditors asking to explore the possibility of making auditing of NBFCs, a prerequisite to registration.

The study of the CRB scandal brings out the level of negative creativity that the man had, and the way he used to defraud thousands of innocent investors.

Works Cited

Press Information Beaureau of India.

Database used: Centre for monitoring Indian economy's prowess vans electronic library.

13

The Ketan Parekh Scam

The financial market of the country was taken by a shocker with the 176-point Sensex crash on the first day of March 2001. It shook the Government of India, the stock markets and the investors all together, for what happened was totally new to the common intelligence of the Indian financial market. Moreover, the union budget tabled a day earlier had been acclaimed for its growth initiatives and had prompted a 177-point increase in the Sensex. This unexpected crash in the stock markets prompted the Securities Exchange Board of India (SEBI) to launch immediate investigations into the unpredictability of stock markets.

The Reserve Bank of India (RBI) ordered some banks to furnish data related to their capital market exposure. SEBI further decided to inspect the books of several brokers who were suspected of triggering the crash. This was after media reports appeared regarding a private sector bank having exceeded its prudential norms of capital exposure, thereby contributing to the stock market volatility.

The Bombay Stock Exchange (BSE) President, Anand Rathi's (Rathi), resignation added to the downfall. Rathi had to resign following allegations that he had used some privileged information, which contributed to the crash. The scam shook the investor's confidence in the overall functioning of the stock markets. By the end of March 2001, at least eight people were reported to have committed suicide and hundreds of investors were driven to the brink of bankruptcy. The scam opened up the debate over banks funding capital market operations and lending funds against collateral security. It also raised questions about the validity of dual control of cooperative banks.

The Man Who Manipulated the Crash

Ketan Parekh was a chartered accountant by profession and used to manage the family business of NH Securities started by his father. He was known for main-taining a low profile. His only dubious claim to fame was in 1992, when he was accused in the stock exchange scam. He was known as the 'Bombay Bull' and having connections with movie stars, politicians and even leading international entrepreneurs like Australian media tycoon Kerry Packer, who partnered Ketan Parekh in KPV Ventures, a $250 million venture capital fund that invested mainly in new economy companies.

Ketan Parekh had created a network of companies, mainly in Mumbai, involved in stock market operations. The dotcom boom contributed to the bull run led by an upward trend in the NASDAQ. The rise of the stocks of information, entertainment and communications stocks all over the world in early 1999 led to a rise of the Indian stock markets as well. The companies in which KP held stakes included Amitabh Bachchan Corporation Limited (ABCL), Mukta Arts, Tips and Pritish Nandy Communications. He also had stakes in HFCL, Global Telesystems (Global), Zee Telefilms, Crest Communications, and PentaMedia Graphics. He selected these companies for investment with help from his research team, which listed high growth companies with a small capital base. According to media reports, KP took advantage of low liquidity in these stocks, which eventually came to be known as the 'K-10' stocks.

Ketan Parekh's company, Triumph International, held these shares in the companies. In July 1999, he held around 1.2 million shares in Global. Ketan Parekh controlled around 16 per cent of Global's floating stock, 25 per cent of Aftek Infosys, and 15 per cent each in Zee and HFCL. The buoyant stock markets from January to July 1999 helped the K-10 stocks increase in value substantially. HFCL soared by 57 per cent while Global increased by 200 per cent. As a result, brokers and fund managers started investing heavily in K-10 stocks. Mutual funds like Alliance Capital, ICICI Prudential Fund and UTI also invested in K-10 stocks, and saw their net asset value soaring. By January 2000, K-10 stocks regularly featured in the top five traded stocks in the exchanges. HFCL's traded volumes shot up from 80,000 to 1,047,000 shares. Global's total traded value in the Sensex was Rs 51.8 billion.

As such huge amounts of money were being pumped into the markets, it became tough for Ketan Parekh to control the movements of the scrips. Also, it was reported that the volumes got too big for him to handle. It was wondered by analysts and regulators that how Ketan Parekh had managed to buy such large stakes. Now with the prices of select shares constantly going up, thanks largely to this rigging innocent investors who bought such shares thinking the market as genuine, were at loss. Soon after discovery of this scam, the prices of these stocks came down to the fraction of the values at which they were bought. The scam burst and the rigged shares came down so heavily that quite a few people in India lost their savings.

The Factors That Helped the Man

According to market sources, though Ketan Parekh was a successful broker, he did not have the money to buy large stakes. According to a report,[1] 12 lakh shares of Global in July 1999 would have cost Ketan Parekh around Rs 200 million. The stake in Aftek Infosys would have cost him Rs 50 million, while the Zee and HFCL stakes would have cost Rs 250 million each. Analysts claimed that Ketan Parekh borrowed from various companies and banks for this purpose. His financing methods were fairly simple. He bought shares when they were trading at low prices and saw the prices go up in the bull market while continuously trading. When the price was high enough, he pledged the shares with banks as collateral for funds. He also borrowed from companies like HFCL.

However, this could not have been possible without the involvement of banks. A small Ahmedabad-based bank, Madhavapura Mercantile Cooperative Bank (MMCB) was Ketan Parekh's main ally in the scam. Ketan Parekh and his associates started tapping the MMCB for funds in early 2000. In December 2000, when Ketan Parekh faced liquidity problems in settlements he used MMCB in two different ways. The first was the pay order route, wherein he issued cheques drawn on BoI to MMCB, against which MMCB issued pay orders. The pay orders were discounted at BoI. It was alleged that MMCB issued funds to Ketan Parekh without proper collateral security and even crossed its capital market exposure limits. As per a RBI inspection report, MMCB's loans to stock markets were around Rs 10 billion of which over Rs 8 billion were lent to Ketan Parekh and his firms.

The second route was borrowing from a MMCB branch at Mandvi (Mumbai), where different companies owned by Ketan Parekh and his associates had accounts. Ketan Parekh used around 16 such accounts, either directly or through other broker firms, to obtain funds. Apart from direct borrowings by Ketan Parekh-owned finance companies, a few brokers were also believed to have taken loans on his behalf. It was alleged that Madhur Capital, a company run by Vinit Parikh, the son of MMCB Chairman Ramesh Parikh, had acted on behalf of Ketan Parekh to borrow funds. Ketan Parekh reportedly used his BoI accounts to discount 248 pay orders worth about Rs 24 billion between January and March 2001. BoI's losses eventually amounted to well above Rs 1.2 billion.

The MMCB pay order issue hit several public sector banks very hard. These included big names such as the State Bank of India, Bank of India and the Punjab National Bank, all of whom lost huge amounts in the scam. It was also alleged that Global Trust Bank (GTB) issued loans to Ketan Parekh and its exposure to the capital markets was above the prescribed limits. According to media reports, Ketan Parekh and his associates held around 4-10 per cent stake in the bank. There were also allegations that Ketan Parekh, with the support of GTB's former CMD Ramesh Gelli, rigged the prices of the GTB scrip for a favorable swap ratio before its proposed merger with UTI Bank. (although the merge later got cancelled).

KP's modus operandi of raising funds by offering shares as collateral security to the banks worked well as long as the share prices were rising, but it reversed when the markets started crashing in March 2000. The crash, which was led by a fall in the NASDAQ, saw the K-10 stocks also declining. Ketan Parekh was asked to either pledge more shares as collateral or return some of the borrowed money. In either case, it put pressure on his financials. By April 2000, mutual funds substantially reduced their exposure in the K-10 stocks. In the next two months, while the Sensex declined by 23 per cent and the NASDAQ by 35.9 per cent, the K-10 stocks declined by an alarming 67 per cent. However, with improvements in the global technology stock markets, the K-10 stocks began picking up again in May 2000. HFCL nearly doubled from Rs 790 to Rs 1,353 by July 2000, while Global shot up to Rs 1,153. Aftek Infosys was also trading at above Rs 1,000. In December 2000, the NASDAQ crashed again and technology stocks took the hardest beating ever in the US. Led by doubts regarding the future of technology stocks, prices started falling across the globe and mutual funds and brokers began selling them. Ketan Parekh began to have liquidity problems and lost a lot of money during that period. It was alleged that 'bear hammering' of his stocks eventually led to payment problems in the markets. The Calcutta Stock Exchange's (CSE) payment crisis was one of the biggest setbacks for him. The CSE was critical for his operation due to three reasons.

One, the lack of regulations and surveillance on the bourse allowed a highly illegal and volatile badla business.

Two, the exchange had the third-highest volumes in the country after NSE and BSE.

Three, CSE helped Ketan Parekh to cover his operations from his rivals in Mumbai.

Brokers at CSE used to buy shares at Ketan Parekh's behest. Though officially the scrips were in the brokers' names, unofficially he held them. He used to cover any losses that occurred due to price shortfall of the scrips and paid a 2.5 per cent weekly interest to the brokers. By February 2001, the scrips held by his brokers at CSE were reduced to an estimated Rs 6-

7 billion from their initial worth of Rs 12 billion. The situation worsened as his badla payments of Rs 5-6 billion were not honored on time for the settlement and about 70 CSE brokers, including the top three brokers of the CSE (Dinesh Singhania, Sanjay Khemani and Ashok Podar) defaulted on their payments. By mid-March, the value of stocks held by CSE brokers went down further to around Rs 2.5-3 billion. The CSE brokers started pressurizing Ketan Parekh for payments. He again turned to MMCB to get loans. The outflow of funds from MMCB had increased considerably form January 2001. Also, while the earlier loans to Ketan Parekh were against proper collateral and with adequate documentation, it was alleged that this time he was allowed to borrow without any security.

By now, SEBI was implementing several measures to control the damage. An additional 10 per cent deposit margin was imposed on outstanding net sales in the stock markets. Also, the limit for application of the additional volatility margins was lowered from 80 per cent to 60 per cent. To revive the markets, SEBI imposed restriction on short sales and ordered that the sale of shares had to be followed by deliveries. It suspended all the broker member directors of BSE's governing board. SEBI also banned trading by all stock exchange presidents, vice-presidents and treasurers. A historical decision to ban the badla system in the country was taken, effective from July 2001, and a rolling settlement system for 200 Group A shares was introduced on the BSE.

The System That Helped the Cause

The small investors who lost their life savings felt that all parties in the functioning of the market were responsible for the scams. They opined that the broker-banker-promoter nexus, which was deemed to have the acceptance of the SEBI itself, was the main reason for the scams in the Indian stock markets. SEBI's measures were widely criticized as being reactive rather than proactive. The market regulator was blamed for being lax in handling the issue of unusual price movement and tremendous volatility in certain shares over an 18-month period prior to February 2001. Analysts also opined that SEBI's market intelligence was very poor. Media reports commented that KP's arrest was also not due to the SEBI's timely action but the result of complaints by BoI.

The steep rise in prices was watched by the SEBI as 'normal' market movements. It ignored the large positions built up by some operators. To worsen the situation it did not ask any questions at all. It had to investigate the matter not as a regulatory body, but as deep-probing agency that could coordinate with other agencies. The loss caused due to the inefficiency of SEBI was to be borne by the innocent people. An equally crucial question was raised by media regarding SEBI's ignorance of the existence of an unofficial market at the CSE. Interestingly enough, there were reports that the arrest was motivated by the government's efforts to diffuse the Tehelka controversy[2].

The People That the System Duped

Ketan Parekh was released on bail in May 2001. The duped investors could do nothing knowing that the legal proceedings would drag on, perhaps for years. Observers opined that in spite of the corrective measures that were implemented, the Ketan Parekh scam had set back the Indian economy by at least a year.

Reacting to the scam, all Ketan Parekh had to say was, "I made mistakes." It was widely believed that more than a fraud, he was an example of the rot that was within the Indian financial and regulatory systems. Analysts commented that if the regulatory authorities had been alert, the huge erosion in values could have been avoided or at least controlled. After all, Rs 2,000 billion is definitely not a small amount—even for a whole nation.

Notes and References

1. *Businessworld*, 16 April, 2001
2. In March 2001, a website, Tehelka.com exposed an alleged corruption racket in defense deals. Many leading politicians, bureaucrats and army personnel were caught on camera indulging in unethical practices. It led to a huge uproar in the media and public, eventually threatening the government's stability. It was alleged that Ketan Parekh's arrest was a ploy by vested interests to divert the nation's attention off the Tehelka controversy.

14

Harshad Mehta Scandal

Harshad Mehta was an Indian stockbroker caught in a scandal beginning in 1992. He died of a massive heart attack in 2001 while the legal issues were still being litigated.

Harshad Mehta: Early Life

Harshad Shantilal Mehta was born in a Gujarati jain family of modest means. His father was a small businessman. His mother's name was Rasilaben Mehta. His early childhood was spent in the industrial city of Bombay. Due to indifferent health of his father in the humid environs of Bombay, the family shifted their residence in the mid-1960s to Raipur then in Madhya Pradesh and currently the capital of Chattisgarh state. An Amul advertisement of 1999 during the controversy over MUL saying it as "The Big

Bhool" (Bhool in Hindi means Blunder) He studied at the Holy Cross High School, located at Byron Bazaar. After completing his secondary education he left for Bombay. While doing odd jobs he joined Lala Lajpat Rai College for a Bachelor's degree in Commerce.

After completing his graduation, Harshad Mehta started his working life as an employee of the New India Assurance Company. During this period his family relocated to Bombay and his brother Ashwin Mehta started to pursue graduation course in law at Lala Lajpat Rai College. His youngest brother Hitesh is a practising surgeon at the B.Y.L. Nair Hospital in Mumbai. After his graduation Ashwin joined (ICICI) Industrial Credit and Investment Corporation of India. They had rented a small flat in Ghatkopar for living. In the late seventies every evening Harshad and Ashwin started to analyse tips generated from respective offices and from cyclostyled investment letters, which had made their appearance during that time.

In the early eighties he quit his job and sought a job with stock broker P. Ambalal affiliated to Bombay Stock Exchange (BSE) before becoming a jobber on BSE for stock broker P.D. Shukla. In 1981 he became a sub-broker for stock brokers J.L. Shah and Nandalal Sheth. After a while he was unable to sustain his overbought positions and decided to pay his dues by selling his house with consent of his mother Rasilaben and brother Ashwin.

The next day Harshad went to his brokers and offered the papers of the house as guarantee. The brokers Shah and Sheth were moved by his gesture and gave him sufficient time to overcome his position. After he came out of this big struggle for survival he became stronger and his brother quit his job to team with Harshad to start their venture Grow More Research and Asset Management Company Limited.

While a brokers card at BSE was being auctioned, the company made a bid for the same with financial assistance from Shah and Sheth, who were Harshad's previous broker mentors. He rose and survived the bear runs, this earned him the nickname of the Big Bull of the trading floor, and his actions, actual or perceived, decided the course of the movement of the Sensex as well as scrip-specific activities. By the end of eighties the media started projecting him as "Stock Market Success", "Story of Rags to Riches" and he too started to fuel his own publicity. He felt proud of this accomplishments and showed off his success to journalists through his mansion "Madhuli", which included a billiards room, mini theatre and nine-hole golf course. His brand new Toyota Lexus and a fleet of cars gave credibility to his show off. This in no time made him the nondescript broker to super star of financial world. During his heyday, in the early 1990s, Harshad Mehta commanded a large resource of funds and finances as well as personal wealth.

By 1990, Mehta rose to prominence in the stock market. He was buying shares heavily. The shares which attracted attention were those of Associated Cement Company (ACC). The price of ACC was bid up to Rs. 10,000. When asked, he used the replacement cost theory as an explanation.

He was alleged to have an expensive lifestyle. Through the second half of 1991 Mehta had earned the nick name of the 'Big Bull', because he was said to have started the bull run.

Mehta made a brief comeback as a stock market guru, giving tips on his own website as well as a weekly newspaper column.

1992 Security Scam

On April 23, 1992, journalist Sucheta Dalal exposed Mehta's illegal methods in a column in *The Times of India*. Mehta was dipping illegally into the banking system to finance his buying. The author explains:

> The crucial mechanism through which the scam was effected was the ready forward (RF) deal. The RF is in essence a secured short-term (typically 15-day) loan from one bank to another. Crudely put, the bank lends against government securities just as a pawnbroker lends against jeweller. The borrowing bank actually sells the securities to the lending bank and buys them back at the end of the period of the loan, typically at a slightly higher price.

It was this ready forward deal that Mehta and his accomplices used with great success to channel money from the banking system.

Making of 1992 Security Scam

A typical ready forward deal involved two banks brought together by a broker in lieu of a commission. The broker handles neither the cash nor the securities, though that wasn't the case in the lead-up to the scam. In this settlement process, deliveries of securities and payments were made through the broker. That is, the seller handed over the securities to the broker, who passed them to the buyer, while the buyer gave the cheque to the broker, who then made the payment to the seller. In this settlement process, the buyer and the seller might not even know whom they had traded with, either being known only to the broker. This the brokers could manage primarily because by now they had become market makers and had started trading on their account. To keep up a semblance of legality, they pretended to be undertaking the transactions on behalf of a bank.

Another instrument used was the Bank receipt (BR). In a ready forward deal, securities were not moved back and forth in actuality. Instead, the borrower, i.e., the seller of securities, gave the buyer of the securities a BR. As the authors write, a BR "confirms the sale of securities. It acts as a receipt for the money received by the selling bank. Hence the name-bank receipt. It promises to deliver the securities to the buyer. It also states that in the mean time, the seller holds the securities in trust of the buyer."

Having figured out his scheme, Mehta needed banks which issued fake BRs (Not backed by any government securities). "Two small and little known banks—the Bank of Karad (BOK) and the Metropolitan Co-operative Bank (MCB)—came in handy for this purpose. These banks were willing to issue BRs as and when required, for a fee," the authors point out. Once these fake BRs were issued, they were passed on to other banks and the banks in turn gave money to Mehta, assuming that they were lending against government securities when this was not really the case. This money was used to drive up the prices of stocks in the stock market. When time came to return the money, the shares were sold for a profit and the BR was retired. The money due to the bank was returned. This went on as long as the stock prices kept going up, and no one had a clue about Mehta's operations. Once the scam was exposed, though, a lot of banks were left holding BRs which did not have any value—the banking system had been swindled of a whopping? 4,000 crore (US$724 million). When the scam was revealed, the Chairman of the Vijaya Bank committed suicide by jumping from the office roof. He knew that he would be accused if people came to know about his involvement in issuing checks to Mehta. M. J. Pherwani of UTI also died in this scandal.

Scandal Exposure and Trial

Exploiting several loopholes in the banking system, Mehta and his associates siphoned off funds from inter-bank transactions and bought shares heavily at a premium across many segments, triggering a rise in the Sensex. When the scheme was exposed, banks started demanding their money back, causing the collapse.

He was later charged with 72 criminal offences, and more than 600 civil action suits were filed against him.

He was arrested and banished from the stock market with investigators holding him responsible for causing a loss to various entities. Mehta and his brothers were arrested by the CBI on November 9 1992 for allegedly misappropriating more than 27 lakh shares (2.7 million) of about 90 companies, including ACC and Hindalco, through forged share transfer forms. The total value of the shares was placed at ₹ 250 crore (US$45.25 million).

His favourite stocks included:

a) ACC
b) Apollo Tyres
c) Reliance
d) Tata Iron and Steel Co. (TISCO)
e) BPL
f) Sterlite
g) Videocon

The extent the Harshad Mehta induced security scam, as the media sometimes termed it, adversely affected at least 10 major commercial banks of India, a number of foreign banks operating in India, and the National Housing Bank, a subsidiary of the Reserve Bank of India, which is the central bank of India. As an aftermath of the Shockwaves which engulfed the Indian financial sector, a number of people holding key positions in the India's financial sector were adversely affected, which included arrest and sacking of K. M. Margabandhu, then CMD of the UCO Bank; removal from office of V. Mahadevan, one of the Managing Directors of India's largest bank, the State Bank of India. The Central Bureau of Investigation which is India's premier investigative agency, was entrusted with the task of deciphering the modus operandi and the ramifications of the scam. Harshad Mehta was arrested and investigations continued for a decade.

During his judicial custody, while he was in Thane Prison, Mumbai, he complained of chest pain, and was moved to a hospital, where he died on 31st December 2001. His death remains a mystery. Some believe that he was murdered ruthlessly by an underworld nexus (spanning several South Asian countries including Pakistan). Rumour has it that they suspected that part of the huge wealth that Harshad Mehta commanded at the height of the 1992 scam was still in safe hiding and thought that the only way to extract their share of the 'loot' was to pressurise Harshad's family by threatening his very existence. In this context, it might be noteworthy that a certain criminal allegedly connected with this nexus had inexplicably surrendered just days after Harshad was moved to Thane Jail and landed up in imprisonment in the same jail, in the cell next to Harshad Mehta's.

Just as the year 2001 was coming to an end, Harshad Shantilal Mehta, boss of Growmore Research and Asset Management, died of a massive heart attack in a jail in Thane. And thus came to an end the life of a man who is probably the most famous character ever to have emerged from the Indian stock market. In the book, *The Great Indian Scam: Story of the Missing Rs 4,000 Crore*, Samir K Barua and Jayanth R Varma explain how Harshad Mehta pulled off one of the most audacious scams in the history of the Indian stock market.

Mehta again raised a furore in 1995 when he made a public announcement that he had paid ₹ 1 crore (USS$ 181,000) to the then Congress President and Prime Minister, P.V. Narasimha Rao, as donation to the party, for getting him off the scandal case.

Death

Mehta was under judicial custody in the Thane prison. Mehta complained of chest pain late at night and was admitted to the

Thane Civil Hospital. He died following a brief heart ailment, at the age of 47, in December 31,2001. He is survived by his wife and two sons.

Mehta died on with many litigation still pending against him. He had altogether 28 cases registered against him. The trial of all except one, are still continuing in various courts in the country. Market watchdog, Securities and Exchange Board of India, had banned him for life from stock market-related activities.

In a letter to *The Economic Times*, Harshad Mehta's widow, Jyoti Mehta, made some interesting, although emotionally-coloured, points. One was that, after all the hullabaloo, her late husband was convicted only in one criminal case. However, she ignores that his name was automatically dropped from other cases after his death. She also says that there was no law then that required him to keep clients' money in a separate account. It is a bizarre claim, since the clients in this case were State Bank of India, ANZ Grindlays and National Housing Bank (NHB), whose cheques were deposited in Harshad's account. Interestingly, ANZ Grindlays had also claimed in 1992 that crediting bankers' cheques to brokers' accounts was 'an accepted market practice', but the government ensured that this preposterous claim was never argued in court, by quietly pushing its dispute with NHB into arbitration. Next, she says, the custodian has coercively impounded the entire family's assets. But the fact is that the wealth and lifestyle they still enjoy was entirely due to Harshad Mehta's questionable methods.

However, Jyoti Mehta does make one valid point. She says that 'all hell broke loose' after the scam and, instead of minimising the damage, the system seemed determined to maximise it. The scam trial, despite a special statute to investigate it, was disorganised. Nobody worked to a goal of sorting out the tangled money trail or to punish the guilty. We have to agree with her when she says, "In any other country, even if my husband was found guilty, by now, he would have been leading a normal life." In India, after a 20-year effort, which seems set to go on for another decade or more, the special court is discussing the possibility of pushing the hearings-now reduced to just one day a week-to the regular sessions court. The only major beneficiaries of the scam of 1992, and all the later ones, have been India's lawyers, whose incomes rose by a factor of 10 or more.

15

UTI Scam

Unit Trust of India (UTI) was created by the UTI Act passed by the Parliament in 1963. For more than two decades it remained the sole vehicle for investment in the capital market by the Indian citizens. In mid- 1980s public sector banks were allowed toop en mutual funds. The real vibrancy and competition in the MF industry came with the setting up of the Regulator SEBI and its laying down the MF Regulations in 1993. UTI maintained its pre-eminent place till 2001, when a massive decline in the market indices and negative investor sentiments after Ketan Parekh scam created doubts about the capacity of UTI to meet its obligations to the investors. This was further compounded by two factors; namely, its flagship and largest scheme US 64 was sold and re-purchased not at intrinsic NAV but at artificial price and its Assured Return Schemes had promised returns as high as 18 per cent over a period going up to two decades.

Fearing a run on the institution and possible impact on the whole market Government came out with a rescue package and change of management in 2001. Subsequently, the UTI Act was repealed and the institution was bifurcated into two parts. UTI Mutual Fund was created as a SEBI-registered fund like any other mutual fund. The assets and liabilities of schemes where Government had to come out with a bail-out package were taken over directly by the Government in a new entity called Specified Undertaking of UTI, SUUTI. SUUTI holds over 27 per cent stake Axis Bank. In order to distance Government from running a mutual fund the ownership was transferred to four institutions; namely SBI, LIC, BOB and PNB, each owning 25 per cent. Certain reforms like improving the salary from PSU levels and effecting a VRS were carried out UTI lost its market dominance rapidly and by end of 2005, when the new shareholders actually paid the consideration money to Government its market share had come down to close to 10 per cent! A new board was constituted and a new management inducted. Systematic study of its problems role and functions was carried out with the help of a reputed international consultant.

Fresh talent was recruited from the private market, organizational structure was changes to focus on newly emerging investor and distributor groups and massive changes in investor services and funds management carried out. Once again UTI has emerged as a serious player in the industry. Some of the funds have won famous awards, including the Best Infra Fund globally from Lipper. UTI has been able to benchmark its employee compensation to the best in the market, has introduced Performance Related Payouts and ESOPs.

The UTI Asset Management Company has its registered office at: UTI Tower, Gn Block, Bandra[2] Kurla Complex, Bandra (East), Mumbai- 400 051. It has over 70 schemes in domestic MF space and has the largest investor base of over 9 million in the whole industry. It is present in over 450 districts of the country and has 100 branches called UTI Financial Centres or UFCs. About 50 per cent of the total IFAs in the industry work for UTI in distributing its products! India Posts, PSU Banks and all the large Private and Foreign Banks have started distributing UTI products. The total average Assets Under Management

(AUM) for the month of June 2008 was Rs. 530 billion and it ranked fourth. In terms of equity AUM it ranked second and in terms of Equity and Balanced Schemes AUM put together it ranked FIRST in the industry. This measure indicates its revenue-earning capacity and its financial strength.

Besides running domestic MF Schemes UTI AMC is also a registered portfolio manager under the SEBI (Portfolio Managers) Regulations. It runs different portfolios for is HNI and Institutional clients. It is also running a Sharia Compliant portfolio for its Offshore clients. UTI tied up with Shinsei Bank of Japan to run a large size India-centric portfolio for Japanese investors. For its international operations UTI has set up its 100 per cent subsidiary, UTI International Limited, registered in Guernsey, Channel Islands. It has branches in London, Dubai and Bahrain. It has set up a Joint; Venture with Shinsei Bank in Singapore. The JV has got its license and has started its operations. In the area of alternate assets, UTI has a 100 per cent subsidiary called UTI Ventures at Banglore This company runs two successful funds with large international investors being active participants. UTI has also launched a-Private Equity lnfrastructure Fund along with HSH Nord Bank of Germany and Shinsei Bank of Japan.

Genesis of the Scam

Liberalisation of the economy immediately led to the liberalisation of the UTI, throwing it to the mercy of the stock market. In 1992, itself the US-64 scheme was changed from a debt-based fund to one linked to equity. In 1992 only 28 per cent of its funds was in equity; today it is over 70 per cent. Further liberalisation was pushed by Chidambaram, as the finance minister of the United Front government, who, in 1997, removed all government nominees from the board of the UTI. Besides, the US-64 does not come under SEBI regulations, its investment details are kept secret (ever depositors cannot know where their funds are being parked) and the chairman has arbitrary powers to personally decide an investment upto a huge Rs 40 crores. Such 'liberalisation' is tailor-made for frauds. Not surprisingly, within one year of Chidambram's liberalisation, in 1998, the UTI crashed, and the new BJP-led government organised a large Rs. 3,500 crore bail-out to prevent default.

It was during this crisis that the new chairman, P.S. Subramanyam, was appointed. Subramanyam was a direct appointee of thug Jayalalitha, who had made his selection a condition for her continuing the support of the then NDA government. Later, though Jayalalitha withdrew from the government, Subramanyam developed close links with the Prime Minister's Office, and corporative big-wigs. Small investor's funds were used to promote big business houses, shower favours to politicians, and invest huge amounts in junk bonds, all for a fat commission. Subramanyam functioned like a fascist, arbitrarily transferring hundreds of senior staff, in order to cover his tracks. He was a key player in the Ketan Parekh scam.

Huge amount of UTI funds were channelled into the infamous K-10 list of Keten Parekh stock, such as Himachal Futuristic, Zee Telefilims, Global Tele, DSQ, etc. The UTI continued to buy these shares even when their market value began to crash in mid-2000, in order to prop up the share values of these stocks. The Trust saw its Rs. 30,000 portfolio (value of stocks) lose half its value within a year since Feb. 2000.

To take just one example on how the UTI operated : In August 2000, much after the software stocks had begun to crash, the UTI bought Rs. 34 crores worth of shares in Cyberspace Infosys Ltd at the huge price of Rs 930 per share. Today the shares have no value and its Lacknow based promoters, the Johari Group, are in jail. But, what is astounding is that it was none other than India's prime minister, Vajpayee, who, as late as Jan.

31, 2001, laid the foundation stone for the Software Technology Park (STP) in Luknow, promoted by this group. (Incidentally the UP government had a 26% share in this STP). Coincidentally, in the four days when the UTI reversed its earlier decision and subscribed to 3.45 lakh shares of Cyberspace, Subramanyam had rung up N.K. Singh (then secretary in the PMO) at least 4 times. It does not take much imagination to link UTI purchases in Cyberspace with Vajpayee. Similar were the investments in DSQ Software, HFCL, Sriram Multitech and others.

Besides, the UTI also invested in junk bonds like Pritish Nandy communications (Rs. 1.5 crores), Jain Studios (Rs.5 crores), Sanjay Khan's Numero Uno International (Rs. 7.5 crores), Malavika Spindles (Rs. 188 crores) etc. This amounted to nothing but handing over people's money (investments) to the rich and powerful. Thereby thousands of crores were siphoned off to big business and prominent individuals, with the UTI chairman, bureaucrats and politicians taking their cuts.

But this was not all. The fraud continues even further. With knowledge that the UTI was in a state of collapse, the Chairman organised a high profile propaganda campaign promoting UTI (spending crores of rupees on the top advertising company, Rediffusion), while at the same time leaking information to the big corporates to withdraw their funds. The Chairman thereby duped the lakhs of small investors through false propaganda, while allowing windfall profits to the handfull of big corporates who had invested in UTI.

So, in the two month prior to the freezing of dealings in UTI shares, a gigantic sum of Rs. 4,141 crores was redeemed. Of this Rs.4,000 crores (97%) were corporate investments. What is more, they were re-purched at the price of Rs. 14.20 per share (face value Rs. 10) when in fact its actual value (NAV—net asset value) was not more than Rs. 8. As a result UTI's small investors lost a further Rs. 1,300 crores to the big corporates.

In fact these huge withdrawals further precipated the crisis. On July 4, 2001 the board of UTI took the unprecedented step of freezing the purchase and sale of all US-64 UTI shares for six months. Simultaneously it declared a pathetic dividend of 7 per cent (10% on face-value), which is even lower than the interests of the banks and post office saving schemes. Such freezing of legally held shares is unheard of—and is like overnight declaring Rs. 100 notes as invalid for some time. In other words the 2 crore shareholders could not re-invest their money elsewhere—and would have to passively see their share price erode from Rs. 14 (at which they would have purchased it) to Rs 8—and get interest at a mere 7 per cent on their initial investments. Fearing a backlash, the government/UTI later announced the ability to repurchase UTI shares at Rs. 10, i.e., at 30 per cent below the purchase price.

Imagine the plight of a retired person who would have put a large part of his/her PF, gratuity etc. in the US-64 scheme, considering it the safest possible investment. Not only has the person's income (interest/dividend) halved overnight, he/she also stands to lose a large part of the investment. So, a person who invested Rs. 1 lakh would now only get back Rs 70,000.

Today, the entire middle class is being robbed of their savings—first it was by the private mutual funds (NBFCs), now by the govt, sponsored mutual fund. Those who gain are the robber barons who run the country's economics, finance, politics.

The middle-classes, affected by these scam, will soon realise the facts and come out of the euphoria of consumerism that has numbed their senses. They will see through the hoax of globalisation/liberalisation, and will turn their wrath on these so-called pillars of society. It is important that this impending explosion be channelled in a revolutionary direction, or else it will be diverted by the ruling elite into fatricidal clashes. The middle-classes are most prone to fall prey to ruling-class propaganda. But life itself is the best educator. Faced with unemployment, loot of their savings, price rise of all essentials, etc. they will no doubt, join the working class and their peasant brethrens in revolt.

Out Trust of UTI Scam

Former UTI chairman P. S. Subramanyam and two executive directors—M. M. Kapur and S. K. Basu—and a stockbroker Rakesh G. Mehta, were arrested in connection with the UTI scam. UTI had purchased 40,000 shares of Cyberspace between September 25, 2000, and September 25, 2000 for about Rs 3.33 crore (Rs 33.3 million) from Rakesh Mehta when there were no buyers for the scrip. The market price was around Rs 830. The CBI said it was the conspiracy of these four people which resulted in the loss of Rs 32 crore (Rs 320 million). Subramanyam, Kapur and Basu had changed their stance on an investment advice of the equities research cell of UTI. The promoter of Cyberspace Infosys, Arvind Johari was arrested in connection with the case, The officials were paid Rs 50 lakh (Rs 5 million) by Cyberspace to promote its shares. He also received Rs 1.18 crore (Rs 11.8 million) from the company through a circuitous route for possible rigging the Cyberspace counter.

Both the Union government and the Unit Trust of India (UTI) have felled to take any action against tainted UTI officials, as well as against corporates exposed by the Tarapore committee way back in January 2002. This is evident from the Action Taken Report (ATR) tabled before Parliament on May 10 about the JPC report regarding the 2001 stock seam. The final JPC report had recommended an enquiry of the secondary market transactions done by UTI in shares of 89 companies identified, by the Tarapore committee. It had also recommended departmental action against UTI officials involved in Cyberspace sea 111. Moreover, Tarapore panel had exposed the deals behind the US-64 crisis and how banks had privy information regarding the ill-health of the scheme. However, in terms of action taken against these findings, both the government and UTI have failed to finalise any proceedings against the accused other than referring a few cases to the Advisory Board of Banking, Commercial and Financial Frauds, a pre-investigative body under the finance ministry. Some of the companies involved in these cases include Global Tele, DSQ Software, Essar Oil, Zee Telefilms, Essar Steel and HFCL. DTI chairman M. Damodaran was unavailable for comment. After the Tarapore committee report unearthed the dubious deals between UTI officials and leading corporates, UTI ordered an audit of the investment decisions taken in 19 firms. But no action has been taken against these companies or against the concerned. UTI officials. The UTI-administrator was informed the government that with reference to civil proceedings against ex-chairman P.S. Subramaniam and other former UTI officials, "UTI is seeking an external legal specialist and further action will be considered on their advice." On UTI's role in the Calcutta. Stock Exchange payment crisis, the government has directed SEBI to intervene in the matter, since UTI has failed, to initiate any action against its former ED, B.G. Daga, who has been indicted, in the JPC report.

16

Fighting Financial Corruption through Multilateral Financial Institutions

It has been widely observed that insufficient domestic resource mobilization and wasteful public expenditures are at the root of the adjustment and growth problems faced by many countries, including especially those in transition to a market economy. To remedy this situation the basic strategy has relied on reforming the design of taxes and their administration, accompanied by efforts to control expenditure waste and fraud. The often less-than-satisfactory outcome of this strategy has led to a growing perception that corruption and its corrosive effects on fiscal performance should also be addressed.

It is difficult, however, to obtain adequate information on corruption because the involved parties naturally strive for concealment. Broadly, on the side of revenue, some indication of the extent of corruption can be obtained by comparing the theoretical yield of taxes and actual collections, but the shortfall could also be caused by other factors such as the poor organization and administration of tax departments. It is also difficult to establish how much corruption adds to expenditures as standards for comparison are not readily available, especially for public goods, while with respect to procurement and contract specifications, practices may vary between the private and public sectors. Such a situation does no facilitate the construction of an analytical framework to explain corruption and to develop ways to control it.

In the literature, three basic factors have been identified as contributing to corruption. The first is the overall level of potential benefits from corrupt behaviour. Benefits refer to the payoffs from evasion in the case of taxes or excessive billing of government expenditures. The second relates to the costs of bribery, or the penalties and sanctions applicable to briber and bribee. The third concerns the bargaining power of officials, or the extent of exclusive discretionary powers in the hands of individual bureaucrats. High tax rates imply high potential benefits from evasion. A poor record of applying sanctions lowers the costs of being corrupt. Considerable discretionary powers vested in the hands of officers confer the means remedies follow readily: lower tax rates; apply adequate penalties more rigorously; and reduce the discretionary powers of fiscal officers, with the last two also applicable in the area of government outlays. These remedies however, may not be adequate. It may also be necessary to address issues concerning the conditions of service and more generally the motivation of fiscal officers.

Obviously, if officers are poorly paid, or become so as a consequence of an adjustment strategy, for example, wage control in a context of massive price increases, they might be more inclined to engage in corruption. Should the top echelons of government be corrupt, there is likely to be a contagion effect on lower levels. This effect could become more pronounced if it is generally perceived that the administrative structures are being used to promote the self-interest of their managements rather than the mandated objectives. The contagion effect may be further stimulated if, as is often the case in such environments, officers view their own career progression to be dependant on the extent to which they compromise with higher levels. Establishing an organizational structure that is less conducive to compromising behaviour, combined with the right incentive structure and the appropriate *esprit de corps,* can help contain contagion effects. It is likely that the payment of a properly designed bonus, especially if emoluments are inadequate, could be a powerful incentive. But, for such a measure to be effective it is essential to reduce corruption at higher levels.

Most of the attempts at formal modelling in the literature have focused on the behaviour of the briber, for example, the tax payer. Less attention has been paid to the behaviour of the fiscal officer, their conditions of service, and their motivation.

One of the building blocks in creating more civilized and productive societies is an effective effort to deal with issues of fraud and corruption. Anti-corruption efforts should not be thought of as some kind of abstract moral crusade of concern only to starry-eyed reformers, but must be viewed in practical terms as an integral component of the fashioning of the frameworks for progress in nearly every sphere of human endeavour.

There has been an extraordinary increase in the worldwide focus on the problems of corruption over the past ten years. The end of the Cold War ushered in a worldwide commitment to democratic institutions, human rights and market economies. At the same time it has come to be recognized that progress in each of these areas depends upon observance of the rule of law And it is widely recognized that an important component of adherence to the rule of law must be strong anti-corruption efforts. In fact, it is clear that a firm devotion to the rule of law is absolutely essential to attainment of all these goals. Clean elections and freedom from fraud and corruption are necessary for functioning democracies. Due process of law must be an integral component of any effort to protect human rights. Protection of property rights through certainty in the law and a truly independent judiciary is a prerequisite to a functioning market economy.

And we have come to realize that much more assurance is needed that loans and grants from multilateral financial institutions (MFIs) are used for the purposes intended and not siphoned off into other unrelated endeavours or to the Swiss bank accounts of crooked public officials or business tycoons.

The true social consequences of this phenomenon for the developing world are perhaps nowhere better stated than in the 1999 annual report of the World Bank, where it is noted: "Corruption and poor governance worsen poverty directly—by diverting resources away from the needy—and indirectly, by harming the climate for private investment, key to growth and poverty reduction." Thus, the stakes are undeniably high for all the worlds citizens and their governing bodies.

There is much tangible evident of the sense of urgency attached to multilateral efforts to combat corruption today. In addition to initiatives within the UN and the World Bank, anti-corruption conventions have been adopted by the OECD and the OAS, and non-governmental organizations such as Transparency International have laboured to raise the profile of these problems around the world.

Indeed, hardly a day seems to go by without disclosure of yet another new scheme, ever more sophisticated and ever more far-reaching, designed to debase the processes of governance and commerce worldwide.

Given the actual dimensions of the problem of corruption, is it any wonder that such a strong commitment to facing up to this problem appears to be coalescing in so many organizations around the world?

Less attention is being paid, however, to the nuts and bolts of anti-corruption efforts—how specifically to combat these activities effectively. I suggest some basic ground rules for dealing effectively with allegations of fraud and corruption on a comprehensive basis.

Of course, MFIs' responsibilities in this area are of a highly specialized nature. While they are not law enforcement agencies, lacking specifically the legal authority to compel testimony or the production of evidence, they are everything but, with equivalent responsibilities to "follow the evidence wherever it leads." MFIs' operations must be completely independent and free from any political influence:

1. They must have the visible full backing of top management so that their status is clearly established vis-a-vis other components of their organization.
2. Their reporting responsibilities must be at the highest level.
3. They must have the ability to report findings without management interference, subject to no intermediate review other than in an advisory capacity.
4. Their mandate must be clearly spelled out and widely circulated, and a proper framework and policy guidelines for their activities must be in place, with particular attention paid to providing an adequate measure of due process to subjects of their inquiries.
5. The head of their operation and all staff must be free from arbitrary removal.
6. They must have freedom to select, hire, promote and discipline necessary personnel.
7. They must be able to seek and obtain adequate resources to carry out their mandate and have the necessary budget and administrative support personnel to accomplish this goal. Their personnel must be experienced and continually trained in state-of-the-art techniques, able to produce litigation-quality work product and combining the multidisciplinary skills of lawyers, investigators, procurement specialists, and forensic auditors. Their

investigations should produce conclusive evidence of misconduct that can withstand scrutiny and attack by experienced opposing lawyers and skeptical administrative tribunals and serve as a basis for senior management to make crucial operating decisions. Management should be kept informed of significant investigative developments while protecting the integrity and security of the MFFs efforts at the same time.

8. A clear distinction must be recognized between the allegations respecting internal and external corruption, as each should call for different responses.
9. Close rapport must be maintained with country law enforcement agencies, which in many cases will be the ultimate customers. In this respect, MFLs should work with the World Bank Institute and organizations such as Transparency International and others to help "spread the gospel" of effective anti-fraud and corruption efforts to other nations. Our UN Task Force "nuts and bolts" recommendations on effective country anti-corruption efforts can provide useful specifics in this regard.
10. Successes must be properly publicized, both to build the credibility of, and support for, MFIs' efforts and to increase the deterrent effect upon others who might be tempted toward improprieties. An incidental side-benefit of such publicity should be an increase in the number of "whistle-blowers" who come forward with vital leads.

Pitfalls

There are pitfalls to be avoided in MFIs' undertakings as well. Some institutions may be tempted to create units to combat fraud and corruption simply by extending the work of existing auditors and human resource managers into these areas, rather than recruiting those with necessary specialized investigative skills.

From time to time, some within the organization will seek to use the institution's investigative units as a "dumping ground" for innumerable intractable miscellaneous management problems within their own organizations. This must be resisted. MFIs will also be obliged to devise techniques to deal with the inevitable attacks upon the professionalism and integrity of their unit's members. Finally, while MFIs must always seek to follow the evidence wherever it leads, special care should always be taken to the see that investigations go no further, based on mere speculation, pure beyond the limits encountered in conventional law enforcement, but the payoff for the worldwide anti-corruption effort will be substantial.

If MFIs and others involved in this effort follow all of hence prescriptions can corruption be eliminated? Of course not. The worst instincts of humankind can never be reversed completely. But designing and following a well thought-out strategy to combat corruption that incorporate elements will both up the ante for wrongdoers and provide much-needed inspiration for those who value good governance.

With so much attention being focused on the high price of official corruption in so many countries around the world today, the timing could not be better for a vigorous international effort to focus more attention on the antidote for this prison in terms of a specific action agenda that will ensure maximum commitment to better the lot of all concerned.

To fail to undertake effective efforts to combat this threat cannot help but frustrate this century's unprecedented opportunity to move toward realizing the positive aspects of economic and political globalization with their promise of progress towards a better quality of life for all.

Sooner or later, by whatever means necessary, today's terrorist threats will be contained. But the absence of threats to our physical being and peace of mind is only a beginning. Any message of quality of life in any country or region must include consideration of the quality of governance in that country and region. In the long run, corrupt rulers cannot provide their consumed with fulfilment of their hopes and aspirations at a price they are willing to tolerate. Sooner or later, citizens worldwide will demand higher standards and more accountability from those who govern them.

17

Indian Premier League Scandals

Indian Premier League (IPL) is a professional league for Twenty20 Cricket Competition in India. It was initiated by the Board of Control for Cricket in India (BCCI). The scams under the IPL have become so complicated, that makes us doubt, if the IPL itself was created for money laundering. The Officials, Politicians, Corporates and Celebrities involved in the IPL are some of the big names in India. Lalit Modi, Sharad Pawar, Praful Patel, Shashi Tharoor, Multiscreen Media—Sony Entertainment Television, World Sports Group, Shahrukh Khan, Preity Zinta, Shilpa Shetty, Raj Kundra and International Management Group are a few names which are connected with the controversial 'IPL'.

Most of the Politicians claimed to be miles away from the IPL, its management and the auction of players in it. Mr. Sharad Pawar and his family claimed that they were no where connected to the IPL or its bidding. However, the true facts were stunning as Mr. Sharad Pawar and his family held over 16% equity in one of the bidders for IPL Cricket Team. The Pawar's own 33.6 lakh shares (out of 2.07 crore shares) in City Corporation, Pune based Construction Company which bid Rs. 1,176 Crore for a franchise in the IPL. The shares of the Pawar family in IPL are held through two companies, namely Lap Finance and Consultancy Pvt. Ltd.

and Namratta Film Enterprises Pvt. Ltd., which are 100% owned by the NCP Boss, his wife Pratibha and daughter Supriya Sule.

Interestingly, Mr. Praful Patel was also named in meddling of the auctioning of the franchises. The Politics and Cricket have always had a connection, visible through the fact that most of the Presidents of BCCI have been from Politics, right from S.K. Wankhede, N.K.P. Salve, Madhavrao Scindia, Sharad Pawar and Ranbir Singh Mahindra. However, IPL and Politics have been controversially related ever since it started.

Controversy became the other name for Shashi Tharoor, who parachuted into the rough and tumble of the Indian Political from the air conditioned and cushy environs of International Diplomacy. He caught the centre of glitz and glamour when he mentored the Kochi IPL Team and also came in conflict with the then IPL Commissioner; Mr. Lalit Modi. Mr. Modi revealed that Thoroor's friend, who later on became his wife, Ms. Sunanda Pushkar had equity stakes in Rendezvous Sports World, which was heading the consortium that owns the Kochi Team. It was later found out that Pushkar had got sweat equity of Rs. 70 Crores in Rendezvous Sports. Although, Mr. Shashi Tharoor claimed that there was no relation between the sweat equity held by Pushkar and his mentoring and campaigning for the Kochi Team, but it was hard to believe since later on he resigned from the cabinet and married Ms.Pushkar.

The Broadcast Deal

In 2008, the World Sports Group bagged the IPL Television rights for a period of 10 years, for a bid amounting to USD 918 million (close to Rs. 4,590 crore approximately) and also promised to spend USD 108 million on the event. A deal was also signed with Multi Screen Media whereby Sony was made the official broadcaster. However, this deal was scrapped two months before the IPL – Season 2. It was reshaped and agreed again, whereby Multi Screen Media agreed to pay USD 1.63 billion for 9 years. The true picture however, could only be guest by information of Income Tax sources, according to which Multi Screen Media agreed to pay the offshore company of World Sports Group, in Mauritius, a facilitation fee of 7.5% of the IPL Contract, which was around USD 80 million (Rs. 450 crore approximately). The details of the payment were, a remittance of USD 15.3 million from Multi Screen Media to offshore company of WSG on April 14, 2009 via Development Bank of Singapore. The other payment of USD 10.276 million was remitted on June 26, 2009 via two separate instalments. The loss of tax to exchequer could well be calculated on the basis of these figures, running into thousands of crores.

Match Fixing Fiesta

Match fixing in the IPL has been an area of major concern for the Government. The Income Tax investigations into the match fixing charges revealed astonishing facts. The report named Samir Thakral to be the front face of Lalit Modi, the phone records of whom showed conversations with bookies involved in betting and match fixing. The possibilities of match fixing and betting in IPL Season 2, which to place in South Africa, were investigated by the authorities. The serious allegations and evidence was filed along with a confidential report by the investigation wing of Income Tax Department to the Ministry of Finance. Several IPL Players are said to be involved and the recording of phone conversations detail the involvement.

Recently the match fixing scandal was busted by the India TV, where the players of IPL 5 were caught on tape talking about manipulating matches by bowling no-balls at a designated stage of the match. The BCCI suspended the 5 crickets namely TP Sudhindra, Mohnish Mishra, Amit Yadav, Shalabh Srivastava and Abhinav Bali. The channel which busted the spot fixing in

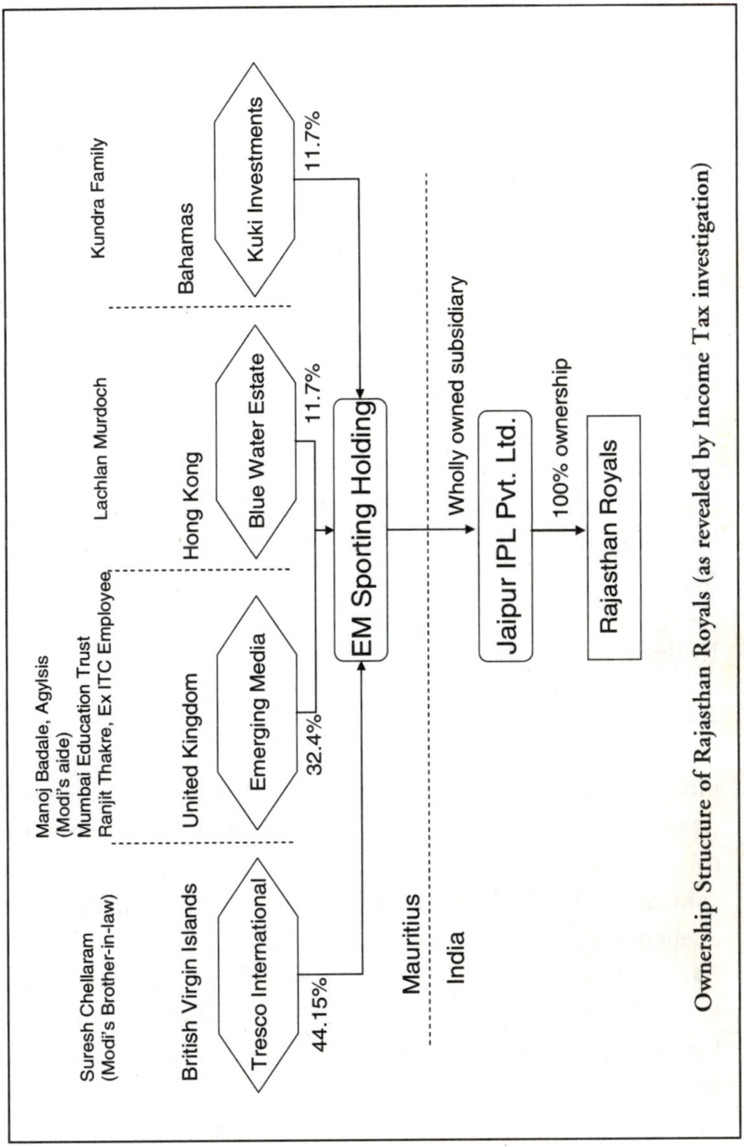

Ownership Structure of Rajasthan Royals (as revealed by Income Tax investigation)

the matches claimed that the spot-fixing is not only prevalent in IPL but first-class matches are also fixed and women play an important role in match fixing.

Team Rajasthan Royals

The glaring example of the misuse of a public functionary office is the silent stake of Mr. Lalit Modi in the team Rajasthan Royals. The enquiry conducted by Enforcement Directorate brought out the FEMA Violations. One Mr. Suresh Chellaram from Nigeria, purportedly the co-brother-in-law of Lalit Modi, controls 25% of the Rajasthan Royals. It is understood that Mr. Chellaram is only representing as a front face of Mr. Modi. Chellaram is said to own 44.15% stake in EM sporting holding, Mauritius, through Tresco International Limited based in British Virgin Islands. Further, UK based Mr. Manoj Badale who is alleged to be an aide of Modi, owns 32.4% in the team through Emerging Media.

Kolkata Knight Riders

The veteran actor Shahrukh Khan was questioned by the enforcement directorate for his involvement in the Hawala and money laundering deals relating to his IPL Team franchise. It came out that his IPL Team franchise is owned by many proxy owners and the ownership is linked to Mauritius based companies. The FEMA and SEBI guidelines and regulations were allegedly flouted by Shahrukh Khan in his team's share transactions. At the time of incorporation of Kolkata Knight Riders, in February 2008, the Red Chilies Entertainment Pvt. Ltd., the entertainment company was by Khan, held 9,900 shares of Kolkata Knight Riders and his wife held 100 shares. However, the shareholding in the franchise changed during the year 2008-9. A Mauritius based company, namely The Sea Island Investment Ltd. was listed as having 50 Lakh shares on 31 March,

2009 and the film star Juhi Chawla Mehta as having 40 Lakh shares out of the total 2 crore shares of Kolkata Knight Riders. The remaining 1.1 crore share capital remained with Red Chilies Entertainment.

Money Laundering

IPL has been the tool for bringing the black money from Swiss Banks to India. The NRIs have been the major stakeholders in the ownership structure of IPL teams. The analysis of team ownership of IPL shows that huge amounts of money have been invested through tax haven countries to avoid complexities of taxation and approvals in India. As per laws in India, an NRI can bring huge amounts of money through his account to invest in India without any barrier or using some simple formalities. Mauritius is the most preferred choice amongst the tax haven countries, from where any amount of money can be brought into India through the NRI bank account and further invest into any other business firms in India (the IPL in this case). This is specifically easier in Mauritius since an investing NRI in Mauritius can bring huge amount of money from any Swiss Bank account to their operating account in Mauritius.

The Income Tax department had received financial details of more than Rs 150 crore in overseas accounts from some tax haven countries of "non- residents" who invested in the IPL. The information regarding investments and remittances to the tune of about Rs 150 crore in IPL media rights has been received from British Virgin Islands and Mauritius. The IPL matches and teams have thus become the effective way to convert "black money" into "white".

Cheergirls

According to a highly confidential income tax source, several high-class (known within Bollywood circles) call girls, who call themselves actresses or models, were allegedly hired or enlisted by a certain personality within the IPL to provide sexual gratification to clients, sponsors, benefactors and patrons. The said allegations are now under investigation by a plethora of agencies. CNN IBN, Headlines Today and Times Now reported that the IT department is investigating and looking into the monies paid to cheer leaders and others who added the glam component. The IT sleuths want to know who hired them, who paid them and how much was paid to them and for what kind of services. It has also come out that many of them were paid huge amounts in cash – something that a body like the IPL should have never done.

Interestingly the controversial IPL has been in the news for all the wrong reasons, since the time it was first started. In May, 2012 two IPL cricketers namely Rahul Sharma from India and Wayne Parnell from South Africa were detained from a "Rave" Party at a hotel in Mumbai. Whereas, the cricketers claimed that they were unaware of the "Rave" Party until the cops raided the scene, they further denied the use of any drugs. In the mean while, the Mumbai Police confirmed that Rahul Sharma and Wayne Parnell tested positive for recreational drugs on the night of the "Rave" Party.

Cricket has been a gentlemen's game ever since it was started playing in the fifteenth century. It has been followed like a religion by the people of India, until the highly-commercialised IPL tournament was launched, which arrives each year, dressed in all its finery. The IPL reiterated the fact that the commercialisation of sports is generally profitable for everyone. But, at the same time, commercialising a sports event, especially through the television has converted sports to yet another form of passive entertainment, rather than a participative one. Statistics have proved that over 80 per cent of Indian children no longer play outdoors or indulge in any sport.

Over Commercialisation of any sport leads to destroying the very spirit of the game and there should be a careful choice between the profits being derived from the same and the love for the sport. There could be a fine balance maintained between making the sport tournaments a hit and retaining the spirit and love for the game.